Life Lessons

Life Lessons

The Case for a National Education Service

Melissa Benn

VERSO
London • New York

First published by Verso 2018
© Melissa Benn 2018

The moral rights of the author have been asserted

1 3 5 7 9 10 8 6 4 2

Verso
UK: 6 Meard Street, London W1F 0EG
US: 20 Jay Street, Suite 1010, Brooklyn, NY 11201

versobooks.com

Verso is the imprint of New Left Books

ISBN-13: 978-1-78873-220-8
ISBN-13: 978-1-78873-222-2 (US EBK)
ISBN-13: 978-1-78873-221-5 (UK EBK)

British Library Cataloguing in Publication Data
A catalogue record for this book is available from the British Library

Library of Congress Cataloging-in-Publication Data

Names: Benn, Melissa, author.
Title: Life lessons : the case for a national education service / Melissa
 Benn.
Description: London ; Brooklyn, NY : Verso, 2018. | Includes bibliographical
 references. |
Identifiers: LCCN 2018027369 (print) | LCCN 2018029215 (ebook) | ISBN
 9781788732222 (United States E Book) | ISBN 9781788732215 (United
Kingdom
 E Book) | ISBN 9781788732208 | ISBN 9781788732222 (US ebk) | ISBN
 9781788732215 (UK : ebk)
Subjects: LCSH: Education and state – Great Britain. | Education – Aims and
 objectives – Great Britain. | Educational equalization – Great Britain. |
 Educational change – Great Britain.
Classification: LCC LC93.G7 (ebook) | LCC LC93.G7 B46 2018 (print) | DDC
 379.0941 – dc23

Typeset in Fournier by MJ & N Gavan, Truro, Cornwall
Printed and bound by CPI Group (UK) Ltd, Croydon, CR0 4YY

For Clyde Chitty: pioneer, inspiration, and friend

Contents

PART THREE: Future Perfect

Introduction

We are at a crossroads. As I write, it is clear that the current Conservative Government has no strategic or even positive vision for the improvement of education for all in England. The drama and drive of the early years of the Coalition Government, shaped by Michael Gove as secretary of state for education, have long faded. For the past few years successive ministers have responded piecemeal to the problems that the 'disruptive transformations' of the preceding years have bequeathed with what one parliamentary report described as a 'disparate collection of small-scale interventions'. Currently, the government's attempts to fix the worst excesses of a previous era are marred by a peculiar determination to wage a low-level war of attrition against the autonomy of our universities and edge our secondary schools back towards the selective practices of a vanished post-war world.

The broad outline of an alternative approach is slowly emerging. Out from the protests against growing inequality and the damaging effects of austerity in the long decade since the 2007–2008 financial crash, has come the rekindling of radical movements and fresh thinking on old problems. In 2015, following the election of Jeremy Corbyn as leader, the Labour Party called for the establishment of a National Education Service (NES) committed to free, cradle-to-grave education. The idea appeared largely symbolic until the publication of Labour's manifesto in response to the snap general election in June 2017 which spelled out some of its education plans in more detail – including the abolition of all university tuition fees, a bold stroke that won it widespread support, particularly among younger voters. A charter of principles, published in the autumn of 2018, outlined a commitment to 'schools rooted in their communities, with parents and communities empowered, via appropriate democratic means ... and policies and practices that will support the emotional, social and physical well-being of students and staff'. The idea of an NES, initially greeted with contemptuous torpor by so many in the educational and political establishment, is now gathering force, with a widespread consultation under way and meetings being held up and down the country.

What exactly is a National Education Service? How, some ask, would it differ from the system as it already exists? The first thing to say is that it is not a proposal for the creation of an overarching institution or, to anticipate *Daily Mail*–type headlines, a rallying call for the Marxist nationalisation of state education (indeed some might argue that this has long ago occurred with central government steadily tightening its grip on education since the late 1980s). A National Education Service has, instead, a fresh promise at its heart: the pledge of genuinely free education over the course of a lifetime: 'cradle to grave' provision. In this alone, it conveys a quite different flavour to our increasingly costly system, unduly concentrated on the school years. Such a service would enshrine a set of guiding principles similar to that of the NHS, whose core values were reaffirmed in 2011 including, among them: a commitment to comprehensive provision free at the point of use; special attention paid to disadvantaged groups; the placement of the individual at the heart of the service; a service that is publicly accountable; and an assurance of professional excellence.

One cannot overestimate the impact and significance of such a similar statement of intent in relation to education, not least in terms of popular perception. From its inception in 1944, free secondary education was established on a very different basis to the free health provision inaugurated by the setting up of the NHS in 1948. While a great advance, free secondary education was essentially a divisive offer to the nation, allocating children to different types of schools before they had reached puberty. In contrast, free health provision was a universal offer to affluent and poor alike. These differing political origins have shaped generations of contrasting public attitudes towards our two great public services: a fiercely loyal attachment to the NHS, even in the hardest of times, compared with an often conditional, critical view of state education, even in the best of times.

A National Education Service seeks to begin to heal that historic divide, to confirm education as a core entitlement, a guarantee from society to each one of its members genuinely to underwrite their intellectual and vocational development. Education must be seen as a collective investment in the public good as opposed to a vehicle solely for the achievement of individual 'aspiration' or 'intergenerational social mobility', which comprise the political emphasis of the past two decades with its corresponding concentration on an ever-more limited, supposedly economically efficient yet apparently unachievable set of outcomes.

As part of that NHS-style entitlement, the NES would knit together disparate services, institutions and stages into a more unifying 'offer' without compromising the distinct character, demands and autonomy of each part. Just as we take for granted that we may visit the GP with a wide range of ailments or go into hospital in times of acute illness or emergency, or feel reassured that one day we might benefit from high-level research in, and treatment of, life-threatening conditions, so the NES will provide us with the education we need, at different times, in different ways, guided by thoughtful, expert educators. Access to free provision from the early years through primary and secondary education to higher and further education, with continuous access to lifelong learning, should be deemed our right as citizens. We should also trust that investment and expenditure decisions reflect the needs of all, not those of the most powerful or influential. A society as rich as ours can afford it; a society as divided as ours cannot afford to continue as we are.

There remains, however, much work to do. And quickly, too. This short work is an attempt to contribute to the conversation that is building around the country, and to sketch out some of the wealth of possibilities contained within the framework of a National Education Service. In doing so, I draw on a progressive tradition that has lost some of its confidence if none of its moral passion over the last thirty or more years, and to develop fresh ideas about the purpose and future direction of our system. It may not be possible to make firm plans for reform without knowing the character or mandate of the next elected government, but we can establish clarity of aims and a clear sense of the pressing problems that face us.

For those with an understandable allergy to acronyms we might instead label it a 'new educational settlement'. Many, whatever their political allegiance, feel a deep uneasiness at the narrowing of the school experience, the marginalisation of whole groups of learners, government meddling in our universities and the barren wasteland that is current further and adult education provision. Those who came to professional and political adulthood over the last twenty years are now questioning the wisdom of many recent reforms, particularly during the Coalition years. These have brought uncertainty, a measure of chaos, and even corruption to our system. They have not, as rashly promised, diminished inequality of outcomes, but instead ushered in what appears to be a more constricted, less imaginative system for all.

This emphasis on the need to build consensus wherever possible is important. Looking at the global scene, it is clear that those countries that have fashioned the most successful educational systems over the past few decades have done so through an often long, involved process of discussion and negotiation. This has led to the eventual creation of high-quality universal systems that are non-selective and publicly supported.[1] And the question of taking one's time to get things right is important. The single greatest error of the Coalition era was its unseemly speed and failure to seek wide agreement, particularly from within the profession, while wilfully destroying some of the more positive aspects of the legacy of previous generations. Anyone interested in forging a fresh vision for the future must not make the same mistakes. I have talked about how the NES should more closely echo the historic objectives of our NHS but, in terms of future reform, we should not underestimate the time and patient negotiations that will be required to shift our system in more genuinely egalitarian and imaginative directions.

So where are we today? What have we achieved over the last seventy years, and on what foundations should the twenty-first-century NES be laid? I begin by briefly looking at three key themes that have shaped our past, continue both to inspire and bedevil today's education system and will need to be resolved within a future NES: first, the continuing battle over selection and the comprehensive principle; second, the back-and-forth arguments over so-called progressive versus traditional education, which have often slowed the development of an approach that is both rigorous and of genuine high quality; and third, the increasing role of the market in our system. Historically speaking, the impact of market forces is a relatively new development, but arguably it is this shift that has had the most dramatic and damaging impact on our schools and now our universities. I then move on to consider how several pressing problems, from growing pressures on school budgets, the government's determination to expand grammar schools and the rogue power of the market are unexpectedly forging a potentially powerful set of alliances for change.

From a better understanding of where we are and how we got here, we can look at what needs to be done. This demands a broad range of objectives and policies. Not all of the ideas I lay out chime with plans put forward by

Labour in its manifesto and charter; some go well beyond their current plans or assumed remit. In the final chapters, therefore, I stress the importance of keeping our eye on the bigger picture: the need to change the terms of the conversation around education, the implications of technological and economic change for learning and the vital importance of working towards the integration of private and state education into a genuinely public system for the twenty-first century.

Throughout, I consider education at all stages and ages from the early years right through to university and adult education. Each sector has its own distinct genesis, structures and problems, and different parts of the system cannot always be neatly linked in terms of analysis or policy prescription. I have tried to bring out both points of commonality and difference where relevant but, perhaps inevitably, the focus is chiefly on primary and secondary education – that part of the system through which everyone must pass.

A final point about vocabulary. When discussing the fee-paying sector, I have chosen to call these institutions 'private schools' for the sake of both linguistic and political clarity. To the great socialist thinker R. H. Tawney, the term 'public school' was 'comically inappropriate'. It also became confusing as genuinely public education expanded during the twentieth century. Personally, I would like to see us talk less about the 'state' system, with all the authoritarian overtones that accompany that word, and instead reclaim the much more open and generous term 'public education' as is commonly used in both the United States and Europe. As for the description 'independent school', favoured by many in the private sector in recent years, while I agree that private schools are at arm's length from society's most pressing problems, this, too, is a misnomer given the large amounts of public subsidy channelled into fee-paying institutions.

Over the past fifteen years, and particularly since the publication of *School Wars: The Battle for Britain's Education* in 2011, I have entered into debate with just about every sector and perspective within English education, including the heads of some of England's major private schools and the leaders of the more-celebrated academy chains. However, one of the privileges of being a campaigner is that those feeling besieged or trying to further new ideas eagerly encourage dialogue with supportive others, so I have been lucky enough to be invited to visit schools all around the country, talk to hundreds of parents, heads and teachers, and take part in numerous gatherings. These have included the vibrant Northern Rocks conference, a gathering of hundreds of teachers held every June in Leeds, and the final conference of the Cambridge Review group in late 2016, an umbrella organisation that brought together dedicated professionals working within primary education. There remain many spaces and places like these where alternative ideas are regularly discussed from the pages of the web campaign group Local Schools Network to the pages of *Forum*, the only journal promoting comprehensive education from ages three to nineteen. *Forum*'s archive provides us with a valuable window on fifty-plus years of educational reform, while continuing to solicit and publish a range of radical voices today. I continue to learn from every one of these enterprises and encounters, each of which has shaped and clarified my own point of view; another reason why *Life Lessons* seems an apt title.

PART ONE

Backstory

1

The Long Road to Reform

Undoubtedly, the education service has markedly improved over the last sixty years. Our young people are better educated, they enjoy greater opportunities than ever before and their aspirations and expectations are higher than we could have dreamed of when we were their age. There is, however, a lot still to be done if we are to fulfil the vision for education outlined in the 1944 Act.

David Bell, Chief Inspector of Schools, 2004

Where to start? While the opening of the first private school, King's College in Canterbury, can be dated back to the year 597 and the earliest university, Oxford, was established around the middle of the twelfth century, our more-democratic institutions of learning have only taken root in far more recent times. Official accounts date the beginning of adult education to the founding of Toynbee Hall in the late nineteenth century, but there is evidence of much political and working-class activity before then. In 1851 the Chartist reformer Bronterre O'Brien opened the wonderfully named Eclectic Institute in Denmark Street in London's Soho, offering adult education classes in English, French, science and maths.

While the Elementary Act of 1870 was the first in a sequence of legislation to underwrite compulsory education in England and Wales (Scotland and Northern Ireland have always had autonomous school systems) it makes sense for our purposes to begin our brief historical survey in 1944 with the establishment of universal free secondary education (up to age 15). This was an important advance that had long been urged by progressive thinkers such as R. H. Tawney, who had published *Secondary Education for All* in 1926.

Although the Act itself made no direction as to the organisation of schools, the decision was made to set up the secondary system along tripartite lines. This sorted children into different kinds of learners, to be sent to three types of school: grammars, secondary moderns and technical colleges. Soon after, largely for reasons of resources, this became a binary system – grammars and secondary moderns – placing the young into two distinct camps: the so-called academic, and those deemed not to be.

This was not necessarily inevitable. Comprehensive education had been debated in progressive circles prior to the Second World War, and the 1938 Spens Report had carefully considered, if not finally embraced, the idea of multilateral schools: that is, comprehensive provision up to the age of 14. However, the Conservatives were wedded to a selective system, as was a powerful strand of Labour opinion represented by such influential figures as R. H. Tawney and 'Red' Ellen Wilkinson, minister of education in the postwar Attlee Government, who wanted to preserve 'a ladder of opportunity' for some working-class children.

The story of the great social divide enshrined in the 1944 Act and its many human and educational consequences has been much told, so I will pick out only a few salient facts. It was clear from the start that the eleven-plus exam – used to divide children at the end of the primary stage and determine entry into grammar school – was (and indeed remains) an unreliable test. It was largely working-class children who lost out, sent to the less-well-resourced schools offering a narrower curriculum with far fewer opportunities to gain qualifications (although there were some inspiring institutions within the dispiriting national model, such as St George-in-the-East, a secondary modern in Stepney, led by the innovative Alex Bloom).

While a few young people from working-class and lower-middle-class homes did spectacularly well in grammars, and found their lives transformed, particularly if they went to Oxbridge (Alan Bennett, Andrew Neil and Margaret Forster are among the more famous names that come to mind), many selective schools were of poor quality. As Adrian Elliot, a former comprehensive head, records in his study of state education since the late 1950s. 'According to the Crowther Report in the late '50s a staggering 38 per cent of grammar school pupils failed to achieve more than three passes at O-level ... Of the entire cohort of sixteen-year-olds at this time, only about 9 per cent achieved five or more O-levels and ... less than half of those who attended grammar schools reached this benchmark.'[1] The historian David Kynaston marks the class divisions within the sector even more starkly:

> By the mid-1950s a middle-class child who had been to a grammar
> was five times as likely to go on to a university as was a child from

an unskilled working-class background who had also been to a grammar; while by the 1960s the 22% chance that a boy from a working-class background would attend a grammar – compared with a 66% chance for a boy from a service-class background – was actually 5% less than it had been in the 1950s.[2]

This may have been one of the many contributing reasons why the grammar/secondary modern divide lasted for such a short period. Protests began building from the late fifties onwards as middle-class parents who resented their children being sent to what were clearly regarded as second-rate schools were joined by researchers who questioned the empirical basis of an 'intelligence' test and progressive campaigners who believed that every child had the right to a broad and balanced curriculum and stimulating teaching. From the early 1960s onwards, these rebellions, harnessed to a Labour Party by now committed to comprehensive education, led to the reorganisation of the school system along largely non-selective lines.

Why do we still know so little, and celebrate even less, the successes of comprehensive education? That a new generation of educational activists and administrators, including anti-grammar Tories and many in the academy and free school movement, now adhere to its principles so hard fought for half a century ago but rarely give it credit is not merely a form of disguised tribalistic discourtesy: it is also the result of a long-standing distortion of the historical record. So much of the history and practice of early comprehensive education has been forgotten or woefully misrepresented in the media and political mainstream and too lazily conflated with sloppy standards, poor discipline and working-class failure summed up in the peculiar phrase, 'the soft bigotry of low expectations'. In one of the more comic examples of the attack-dog genre, the writer Tony Parsons jibed that 'as a start in life going to a comprehensive is the equivalent of dying on the Somme'.

In fact, the advent of comprehensive education meant that millions of children no longer faced demoralising, life-altering tests at the tender age of eleven. Many were given a chance, for the first time ever, to study a much broader range of subjects, and go on to university. Comprehensive reform carved out new and promising paths as definitively as the grammars did for the lives of a previous generation. For Brian Simon, the educational historian and leading reformer:

> the concept of a common curriculum for all … was a major objective of the whole comprehensive reform movement of the 1960s and 1970s. This movement was primarily concerned to prevent shutting off access to full life opportunities for considerable proportions of the nation's youth.[3]

Peter Housden's study of schools in Market Drayton, Shropshire, in the mid-sixties traces the tangible impact of the change. In 1958–60, just 17.5 per cent of the pupils of the town's grammar and secondary modern schools had left school 'with a meaningful basket of qualifications'. In 2014, the equivalent figure for the Grove, the comprehensive that replaced the grammar and secondary modern, was 55 percent. In 1958–60, 6 per cent of pupils had achieved at least one A Level pass; in 2014, 22 per cent did so.[4] These figures are reflected on a national basis: the number of students in education at age seventeen grew from 31 per cent in 1977 to 76 per cent in 2011 and those achieving a degree rose from 68,000 in 1981 to 331,000 in 2010, an almost five-fold increase.[5]

Statistical evidence is useful, but the meaning of the change resonates far more powerfully at a human level. Reviewing his career in secondary education, the pioneer teacher and campaigner Clyde Chitty has spoken of how 'appalled' he was at his first placement in the sixties at a secondary modern in Penge, south London, where 'because they'd failed the eleven-plus, [the boys] were treated like dirt and that upset me'.[6] Chitty saw how selection permeated the attitudes of everyone in the system, from children through to parents, teachers, politicians and the media. Chitty compares this to his later experience at a Leicestershire comprehensive, Earl Shilton, where there was much more openness, creativity and achievement:

> We insisted that boys did typing and girls did metalwork and woodwork, and that was good. That was new. A large [percentage of children stayed beyond sixteen] ... in my last year four of my A level history class got into Oxford and they were girls and that was tremendous.[7]

In Chitty's view, the foundational belief of comprehensive education, and his own practice, is that 'you have to think that every child in front of you has amazing ability'.

So much more could have been made – and still could – of the key principle of 'universal educability': the idea that all, not just a chosen few, deserve the broadest, the best education. The history of our system is, in some ways, the story of the consistent underestimation of the abilities and talents of most young people. It explains not just the latent social bias underlying selective practices but the racism of the '60s and '70s that led many black parents to start up their own supplementary schools, in order to provide a more stimulating schooling, and the unconscious (or indeed conscious) sexism that, not so long ago, deemed girls unfit to master maths or science subjects and which still channels many working-class girls into caring or service work. Children with 'special needs' are still too often considered an expensive problem that needs expunging from mainstream schooling.

As I discuss in the next chapter, the debate about selection has been reignited by the current prime minister, Theresa May, and some key allies, who are keen to take us back to that failed post-war world. It is therefore more important than ever that progressive political leaders reflect intelligently on the huge gains set in train by the reforms of the '60s and '70s while at the same time showing a nuanced understanding of mistakes made and wrong turnings taken along the way. Within this, it should not be forgotten that today's widespread commitment across the political spectrum (or, at the very least, lip service paid) to the idea of all children getting a shot at an 'academic education' is the *direct result* of comprehensive reform. It changed our deepest attitudes for the better and should be built on, not dismantled.

However, at the same time as incremental moves were made towards fostering more radical perceptions of human possibility, there have been, over the past half century, perennial calls for action in the opposite direction: a constant agitation to return education to its most traditionalist forms and methods. An early intervention of this kind can be found in the *Black Papers*, a series of articles published in the *Critical Quarterly* from 1969 to 1977, with contributions from writers such as Kingsley Amis, Iris Murdoch and the London comprehensive head and later Conservative MP Rhodes Boyson. *Black Papers* authors took issue with the phasing out of selective tests for secondary education and the student sit-ins of the late sixties, but they became synonymous with a rejection of so-called 'progressive education' and the call for a return to more conventional methods of teaching and strict discipline.

The traditionalism of the more immediate period has drawn inspiration from two distinct sources: England's private and grammar schools, and the charter school movement in the United States. Influential figures from Labour's Andrew Adonis to the Conservative Michael Gove have made clear their belief that comprehensive education should model itself on the attitudes and atmospheres of selective and private education. During the Coalition years (2010–2015) the US charter school movement, which inspired much of the academy and free school revolution – with its focus on a strong knowledge and test-based curriculum often backed up with draconian behaviour policies – took centre stage in fierce debates. The movement attracted a kind of evangelical fervour on both sides of the Atlantic but one little noted feature linked both perspectives: neither advocated broader social and economic change or a more integrated, equal educational system. Instead, reform was predicated on a version of separate but not-at-all-equal. Far from being a political problem, the private sector was – and is – considered a model that the new 'independent state schools' have sought to emulate, albeit with diluted resources: an approach sometimes summed up in the catch line 'culture not cash'.

In the early years of the Coalition, something of the flavour of the Black Papers re-emerged. Robert Peal, a young teacher, attracted attention with his polemic *Progressively Worse: The Burden of Bad Ideas in Our Schools*, which placed the failure of modern English education firmly at the door of progressive 'experiments' in schooling, the supposed prioritising of skills over knowledge in state schools, and alleged liberal enabling of rowdy behaviour in our classrooms. Education Secretary Michael Gove also spoke of the 'progressive betrayal' which had actively harmed working-class children's chances. Shortly afterwards, the Coalition Government implemented a number of what many believe were backward-looking changes, including the compulsory imposition of phonics in primary schools, major revisions of the primary curriculum and the content of GCSEs, including the removal of coursework and 'speaking and listening' modules, and of A levels.

Yet the story of progressive methods is often the story of our school system at its best and boldest. We can find its origins in the impressive work of the philosopher John Dewey: in particular his conviction that students need to be engaged in their own learning and that school should be a preparation for active citizenship. The 1931 Haddow Report on primary education argued that 'a good school is ... not a place of compulsory instruction, but a community of old and young, engaged in learning by cooperative experiment' and that 'the curriculum is to be thought of in terms of activity and experience rather than of knowledge to be acquired and facts to be stored'. The Plowden Report of 1967 emphasised the multiple ways in which knowledge can be discovered and anchored in a young person's mind, that learning can be a kind of play rather than a grim grind, and that the teacher should be trusted to decide which approach to adopt at any given time.

Many of these ideas have passed into common currency and practice, if not political rhetoric, just as the wilder practices of some allegedly 'child-centred' philosophies have been rightly consigned to oblivion. It is also true that, within many classrooms, progressive approaches have long co-existed with the more fruitful elements of traditionalist methods: emphasis on mastery of key skills, deep knowledge, the judicious use of homework, and informal and continual revision of facts in order to anchor what has been learned. If one compares the methods of the pioneer teacher-educator Winifred Mercier, working in Manchester and Leeds in the early twentieth century, with that of the contemporary teacher and head and influential blogger Tom Sherrington, author of *The Learning Rainforest*, there are far more points of continuity and similarity than difference: in the work of both, one finds a commitment to a complex mix of the acquisition of knowledge and the development of skills, both sustained, hour by hour, week by week, by the enthusiastic engagement and autonomous judgement of highly skilled professionals.

The potentially most significant, and worrying, development of the past seventy years is relatively recent: the semi-marketisation of our education system, including, since 2010, in higher education. The introduction of tuition fees under New Labour in 1998, which were subsequently raised by successive Labour governments and took a sharp upward turn after 2010 under the Coalition, has turned England into one of the most expensive higher education systems in the world.

Other changes followed in the wake of this move. Like schools from the late 1980s onwards, universities were set in competition with each other, institutions tested and judged through the results of the Research Excellence Framework and latterly the Teaching Excellence Framework, both creating long paper trails and the deployment of dubious metrics. Higher education now has its own league tables, ranking everything from student facilities to rates of graduate employment and earnings. Furthermore, the replacement of the block grant by the fee structure has also enabled the opening up of the market to new providers. A host of private institutions have grown up, some charging double the fees of English universities and attracting wealthy foreign and domestic students with the lure of Oxbridge-style tutorials and liberal arts curricula.

If one side effect of the move to the loan system has been that universities have been protected from the chill winds of austerity, it has also dangerously shifted the balance of interests away from both students and junior and middle-ranking staff. Over the past few years, the salaries of senior management, particularly vice-chancellors, have rocketed and universities have indulged in an array of luxury, even vanity, projects – new buildings, superstar academics – designed to lift a university's place in the rankings. At the same time, employment conditions for many academic staff have become increasingly precarious, with junior lecturers and Phd students working in casualised, insecure and low-paid roles. As Becky Gardiner, Goldsmiths lecturer observes,

> Successive governments, enthusiastically aided by overpaid senior management drawn from outside the university sector, have

turned higher education into a utilitarian and consumer-driven activity that students buy in exchange for skills for the job market. The raid on pensions fits this pattern – it is an attempt to shift the risk of volatility in the market from the employer to the individual, to pave the way for further privatisation and rid universities of any remaining sense of responsibility for the long-term health and dignity of their workforces. [8]

The opening up of schools to a market-led approach can be traced back to the Great Educational Reform Act three decades ago. The 1988 Act brought in new kinds of schools and league tables while at the same time imposing fresh layers of central government regulation, principally in the form of a cumbersome national curriculum. Suddenly, schools were to be in competition with each other, assessed through the publication of performance data. Open enrolment meant that geographical catchment areas, the traditional basis of school intake, were weakened; parents could, in theory, act as 'consumers' and move their children from school to school. In *School Report: The Hidden Truth About Britain's Classrooms*, published in 2000, the *Guardian* journalist Nick Davies examined, in fine detail, the ways in which the policy enabled white flight and middle-class desertion of previously mixed schools in one area of Sheffield.

In her new book, *The Best for My Child: Did the Schools Market Deliver?*, the education journalist and campaigner Fiona Millar describes how her local primary school in north London, at which she was a parent and governor, was judged inadequate by Ofsted and performed badly in the league tables. As a result, it was abandoned by large numbers of middle-class families although some, like Millar's, stayed and fought to make the school better. While she cautiously welcomes some aspects of the new accountability, including the compilation of data on pupil and school achievement, Millar points out that comparing schools 'like for like' was never fair, and still isn't, given the vast discrepancies in school geography, intakes and funding. Schools that attract higher achievers through overt or covert selection inevitably produce better results, leading parents with educational 'know-how' or spare capital (which allows them to buy into a desirable catchment area) flock to them. This version of parental choice benefits only a minority, but intensifies class and ethnic segregation and, by depriving many local schools of a genuine mix of pupils, further drags down supposedly poor-performing schools.

The Conservatives also supported the opening of twenty city technology colleges in the late eighties: independent state schools free of local authority 'control' run by sponsors and attractive to ambitious families seeking a better deal within the system. After 1998, New Labour employed the same model to promote its academy programme, seeking private and corporate sponsors to take over or start up schools in disadvantaged areas on the grounds that private energy, and capital, generate more dynamism than representative local government. By March 2010 there were 203 academies open in 83 local authorities, and a further 100 were planned to open in 2010.[9]

If New Labour justified its controversial academy scheme on grounds of efficiency trumping democracy, the 2010 Coalition put the entire model on fast forward. David Cameron's government was greatly influenced by the emergent Global Educational Reform Movement (GERM), the attempt to replace and improve existing 'public' schools with semi-private schools and, in some cases, full blown for-profit models. In the early years of the Coalition, Education Secretary Michael Gove lauded the achievements of charter schools in America and New Zealand, free schools in Sweden and, of course, free schools and academies here.

Some charter schools in the United States were originally set up to pioneer innovative methods of teaching, although as time went on charter schools appeared to rely on, and largely promote their success in terms of, the results of standardised tests. However, Diane Ravitch, one of the most prominent anti-charter school campaigners in the US, accurately pinpointed the underlying politics at play. The charter school movement, she asserted, set out to prove that

> traditional public [i.e.] state schools are bad; their supporters are apologists for the unions ... [meanwhile] those who advocate for charter schools, virtual schooling, and 'school choice' are reformers; their supporters ... are championing the rights of minorities ... they are the leaders of the civil right movement of our day.'[10]

Allowing for some variations in England's political DNA, this neatly sums up the proto-egalitarian, fervent flavour of the argument in England. Structural reform was also justified by alarmist reports of England's flailing position in the PISA (Programme for International Student Assessment) tables for student achievement.

Under the Coalition, the academy model was used to initiate the biggest revolution in school structures since 1944, with up to half of the secondary estate, and a significant number of primaries, either persuaded or forced to convert, at huge public cost. Academies and free schools were established through individual contracts between the education secretary and each academy trust – in many cases a handful of 'members' who, following a start-up business model, are often friends or part of the same family. Academy trust leaders include among them prominent business people or even ministers, separately responsible for education policy on a national basis. As academy 'members' these individuals are given the right to agree the trust's constitution, appoint and sack other trustees, and granted control (at a local level) of budgets that run into hundreds of millions of pounds.

Private control of public education in the UK has not yet reached the level of the United States, where, in the words of the writer David L. Kirp, many charter school chains have become 'playthings of the superrich'.[11] Yet, as in the US, no definitive claim can actually be made for the educational or results-based superiority of the independent state school model over the 'old' maintained model: inequality remains a key shaping factor in school performance.[12]

2

Emerging Crises, Emerging Consensus

Only a crisis – actual or perceived – produces real change. When that crisis occurs the actions that are taken depend on the ideas that are lying around.

Milton Friedman, 1982

Three brief snapshots of a very English-style rebellion:

1. England's school funding crisis has deepened, as costs rise steeply and government revenue remains fixed. During the June 2017 general election, the National Union of Teachers' website campaign 'Schools Uncut' starkly illuminated the impact of budget cuts, area by area, school by school. Many parents rallied to offer support after direct appeals for help from head teachers. Some set up specific anti-cuts campaigns. Heads began to speak openly of the desperate situation they faced including bigger classes, the shaving of budgets for arts subjects, crumbling buildings and the need to make redundancies. According to

a post-election survey conducted by the polling group Survation, the issue of school funding led to 10.4 per cent of voters, or 795,000 people, changing their minds about who to vote for. In November, 2017, 5,000 head teachers, from Cumbria to Cornwall, representing twenty-five counties and millions of pupils, delivered a letter to Downing Street ahead of the winter budget, demanding sufficient money to do their job.

2. In early 2018 I listened to Geoff Barton, former head of an outstanding comprehensive in Suffolk and recently elected head of the Association of School and College Leaders (ASCL), deliver an impassioned speech to a gathering of head teachers from around the country. Barton displayed controlled anger at the pressures too many of his colleagues were put under in today's fragmented, punitive landscape. Too many heads were 'compliant, fearful, timid, terrified' he said, and he called for colleagues to display 'ethical leadership', criticising those schools that excluded vulnerable or special needs children, a process known as off rolling, in order to boost results and win local admissions turf wars. Barton suggested that schools stop displaying the ubiquitous banners celebrating Ofsted judgements and instead 'put banners outside schools stating what we do well. Let's tell the stories of our schools more boldly, more proudly. Let's put Ofsted back in the box.'

3. It was spring 2018, but the weather was suddenly biting. Thick snow fell in parts of the country. Nonetheless, thousands of lecturers at universities and colleges around the country came out on strike in protest at plans by Universities UK to institute new pension arrangements that would cut

staff pensions by several thousand pounds a year. The lecturers stood firm, refusing Universities UK's first offer. Reports from up and down the country suggested that the talk on the picket lines, and unofficial seminars, was less about the pension issue than about all the other things that were going on in universities: the precarious conditions of work, overcrowded lecture theatres and seminar rooms, and the huge gap in salaries between management and staff.

I could add many more examples of a system under severe strain. In the early months of 2018 there were reports that teachers were having to go part-time in order to get their marking done. Thousands of parents threatened to withdraw their children from SATs tests in the summer of that year in protest at excessive testing in primary schools. In that same month, parents of children with special educational needs launched a legal challenge to cuts to local authority budgets, following reports that children who could not be supported were being taken out of school. At the Easter conference of the National Union of Teachers, teachers reported that parents are regularly being asked to contribute to the costs of essential items at school – books, art materials – and that they themselves were having help children living in extreme poverty, with clothing, food and even temporary loans. In April 2018, Peter Horrocks, vice-chancellor of the Open University (OU) – the once-iconic institution of adult education – was forced to resign after putting forward proposals for swingeing cuts and speaking disdainfully of OU teaching. A few weeks later, Sir David Carter, the national schools commissioner, stepped down, two and a half years before his contract was due to expire, with much speculation as to whether this was because of tensions and failings within the fast-expanding academy system. As summer exams approached, press reports focused on alarming levels of stress among teenagers taking GCSEs and A levels.

Politics is a funny, unpredictable beast. For a long time, a set of ideas can feel unchallengeable. Opponents are cast as malcontents, dreamy idealists, self-interested or simply stuck in the past. Then, suddenly, it is as if a dam breaks: existing certainties and long-held assumptions crumble. New ideas (some of which can indeed draw on, but not seek to imitate, the past) pour forth and fresh initiatives and institutions are created. We may have reached such a moment. As I write, senior figures from across the political and educational world call regularly for a fundamental debate on the future direction of our education system.[1] From within these varied protests and demands lie the fruitful beginnings of a shift in public opinion and a broad consensus for reform on a number of related issues.

First, it is now clear that, despite periodic attempts by Theresa May's government, encouraged by a stubborn few on the Tory backbenches, there is very little appetite for expanding selection – the testing of children in order to sort them into different institutions at secondary level. While the law prohibits the creation of new selective institutions, places in the country's 163 grammar schools have grown steadily over the past decade – the equivalent of building eleven new schools – and the government has signalled its intention to continue its support for this process. In May 2018, it announced a £50 million fund to facilitate the expansion of selective schools over the year 2018/2019, with the promise of millions more to come.

However, as I argued in the last chapter, the comprehensive principle has taken far deeper root than many recognise, even as those on the political centre and right who now embrace it purvey more traditional ideas about what constitutes a good education. There may even be considerable if, as yet, unharnessed support for the final phasing out of the eleven-plus, with its separation of children into different institutions, in order to create a fully comprehensive system.

We can, in part, trace this change of heart back to the rise of modernisers within the Conservative Party after David Cameron's election as leader in 2007. Influential Conservative figures, such as David Willetts, then frontbench spokesman on education and employment in the pre-Coalition years, acknowledged the 'overwhelming evidence that such academic selection entrenches advantage, it does not spread it'. The academies and free school revolution post-2010 further consolidated support for comprehensive education among many Conservatives. Many free schools and academies today operate under the strapline 'success without selection' or, more ambiguously, a 'grammar-style school for everyone'.

However, when Theresa May took office in July 2016, she was determined to reshape conservatism in a more populist, pseudo-egalitarian fashion than her gilded Conservative predecessors. 'We will do everything we can to help anybody, whatever your background, to go as far as your talents will take you,' she declared on the steps of Downing Street on taking office as prime minister. For May and her coterie of advisers, the principal policy tool proposed was the expansion of selective education: the fabled route to 'social mobility' of the post-war years.

Labour opposed the plan strongly, under the rubric 'Education Not Segregation'. When in March 2017 the chancellor, Philip Hammond, announced a budget of £320 million to introduce a wave of new free schools that would be allowed to select on academic ability, the shadow education secretary, Angela Rayner, denounced it as a 'vanity project,' claiming that there 'is no evidence to suggest it will help children move from socially deprived backgrounds ... It's a dogma ... opening new grammars is not about giving places to local children that need those schools, it's about sucking money out of the current state public sector.'

Of even greater significance was the fact that the prime minister's proposals were met with almost universal condemnation from the education world, including many influential figures in the free school and academy movement. In the autumn of 2016 and spring of 2017, as chair of Comprehensive Future, a group committed to phasing out the eleven-plus and implementing fair admissions, I took part in a number of debates and found myself sharing platforms, and agreeing, with senior figures in the Coalition-era educational establishment. Implacably opposed to the eleven-plus they saw it as an unjust and premature test that harmed the chances of poorer children who they passionately believed should have access to the same academic education as their better-off peers. Among the prominent figures opposed to the expansion of grammars was the then chief inspector of schools Michael Wilshaw, and senior leaders from the influential organisation Teach First, the academy chain ARK, and the Educational Policy Institute, a think tank led by former Liberal Democrat MP and Coalition minister David Laws.

For the first time in half a century, support for the

non-selective route had shifted to the centre ground and it was cheering, if a little disorienting, after years of hostile commentary, to read positive accounts of the achievements of comprehensive education in the mainstream press. After the Conservatives' narrow victory in the 2017 election, it seemed as if the question was settled – selection was not to be expanded. Within months, however, Education Secretary Justine Greening, who was notably lukewarm towards the policy, was replaced by Damian Hinds, widely believed to be more enthusiastic. According to Ed Dorrell of the *Times Educational Supplement*, 'The idea of grammar schools … is in the very DNA of the Conservative Party. Although David Cameron and Michael Gove managed to stamp on it, they never killed it off. Now, with the party in the hands of a clique of right-wing Brexiteers, it has returned to the fore.'[2]

The Conservatives' continued determination to push on with creating more selective places throws down a challenge to opposition parties. The evidence of the injustice and inefficacy both of selection, and the 'wild west' of unfair admissions policies, continues to grow.[3] Labour, which proposed and piloted comprehensive reform more than half a century ago, seems the logical party now to propose the gradual phasing out of all tests at eleven and progressive reform of school admissions. Any party prepared to do that could command the widespread support of many working in education, as well as many anxious families.

Second, it is clear that the market is failing to foster and sustain a better education system and is, in many ways, damaging the quality of our schools and universities.

In 2010, mass academisation and the introduction of

free schools were hailed as the beginning of a bold refashioning of our school system. Free schools, we were told, were giving parents greater choice and poor children a shot at a first-class education. Those who raised concerns were roundly condemned, in often intemperate terms.[4] Academisation would, we were assured, lead to higher achievement.

There is now increasing scepticism at the ability of the market to deliver a strong and stable educational landscape. According to the keen-eyed educational commentator Laura McInernty, the 'academy dream is in free fall'. Vulnerable schools are left to flounder when failing multi-academy trusts [MATs] give up the ghost of sponsorship, as happened in 2017 when the Yorkshire Wakefield Academies trust handed back a group of schools to the local authority. There are many other problems in the newly fractured landscape, including the dramatic variability in performance between chains, premature expansion of MATs, a lack of suitable sponsors and the sudden appearance of 'orphan' schools that no one will take on (informally known as a SNOW: Schools No One Wants) in the academy transfer market – a failure of local accountability and symptomatic of a lack of engagement with parents.[5]

Political concern over the financial arrangements governing academies and MATs has grown in recent years. A 2014 special report for the Commons Education Select Committee declared that 'conflicts of interest are common', adding: 'There is a broader sense that the academy system lacks transparency.'[6] Meanwhile, the Public Accounts Committee (PAC) found that 'individuals with connections to both academy trusts and private companies may have benefited personally or their companies may have benefited from their position when providing the trust with goods and services'.

In March 2018, the PAC reported that failures within MATs and inadequate financial scrutiny are costing the Treasury large amounts of public money. Government controls over 'related party transactions' (amounting to £120 million in the year ending August 2016 alone) are currently 'too weak to prevent abuse' and it has no power over the unacceptably high level of salaries paid to senior members of trust staff. In 2015–16 there were 102 instances of trustees being paid salaries in excess of £150,000. The PAC report condemned these 'unjustifiably high salaries' that could

> be better spent on improving children's education and support-ing frontline teaching staff, and do not represent value for money. Staff costs represent a substantial proportion of a school's costs already [over 70 per cent], so large increases in salaries, when overall funding is not increasing at the same rate add to the finan-cial pressures faced by schools.[7]

One of the ostensible aims of bringing the private and charitable sector further into state education was to foster innovation. Instead, there is a growing realisation, across the political spectrum, that the mix of market values and neo-traditional practices is leading to a harmful narrowing of the educational experience from the early years through to university.

In many nursery settings, the new official emphasis on literacy and numeracy is forcing out play-based learn-ing. The Royal Society, the Commons Education Select

Committee and the Royal Society for Arts have joined parents and teachers in expressing concern at over-testing in the early years. A recent National Education Union study found that children as young as two and three are being sorted by 'ability' in nursery classes, and more than half of all children in the final year of primary education in England received a letter in the summer of 2016 declaring that they were not 'secondary ready' – in effect, that they had failed the primary phase.[8]

Speaking at the opening session of the International Symposium on the Teaching Profession in Berlin, OECD chief Andreas Schleicher pointed out that the UK now tops international league tables in the 'prevalence of memorisation, of rehearsal, routine exercises, drill and practice and/or repetition', but comes bottom in the 'prevalence of elaboration, reasoning, deep learning, intrinsic motivation, critical thinking, creativity, non-routine problems'. The campaign group More Than a Score argues that 'children in England are some of the most tested in the world … National standardised tests used to rank and judge schools reduce children to statistics. This is grossly unfair.' Some schools list all their children by test and exam scores; at one point it was even suggested that every GCSE candidate in the country should be individually and publicly ranked in terms of their results.

Even the chief inspector of schools, Amanda Spielman, has expressed concern at the way both the primary and secondary curricula are being narrowed in favour of teaching to the test. At primary level, 'schools' understandable desire to ace the English and maths SATs can sometimes compromise a full and varied curriculum'. At secondary level, Spielman says, there is 'a fundamental misunderstanding of the purpose of Years 7 to 9. Just under half of the secondary schools we visited were reducing key stage three to just two years, forcing children to drop important subjects, such as history, music and art, as early as thirteen [and a] large proportion of lower-attaining pupils have a substantially reduced curriculum compared to their peers. Our research found that a wide group of lower-attaining pupils had no opportunity whatsoever to study some arts and Ebacc subjects, such as languages or a humanity, as the school directed them onto a pathway that excluded the subject as an option, in some cases from twelve.'[9]

It is not so much testing as the impact of market-style competition and top-down government control that many now believe to be damaging the undergraduate experience. According to *Observer* commentator Kenan Malik, 'When the satisfactions of students-as-customers become the main metrics by which higher education is judged, then we have a problem.' Malik neatly illustrated the shift in ethos through the decades. Compare, he said, the Robbins Report of 1963 which declared 'the search for truth [as one of the] essential functions of higher education institutions' with the 2010 Browne Inquiry view that 'higher education matters ... because it ... helps produce economic growth, which in turn contributes to national prosperity'.

Such sentiments were echoed in an open letter written in response to the government's 2015 green paper *Fulfilling our Potential: Teaching Excellence, Student Mobility and Student Choice* by the vice-chancellor of Sheffield University, Sir Keith Burnett.

> The change in relationship from student member of a university to a customer is profound, and one which we in Sheffield have

actively resisted. When I was asked at my interview for my present role whether I thought of students in this way I said 'No'. I said no because I had always thought of my students as … my students. *This is not equivalent to any other relationship. It is closer to a family friend role than a consumer relationship.* It means that it is more important to me … If universities shape education to receive the payback of an enhanced NSS score, we could risk harming our students' long-term interests as we focus on satisfying rather than pushing a student to be what we feel they could be. Our duty is to do what is right, not what is easy.[10]

Hardly a week now passes without a senior academic expressing deep concern at what has happened to our universities. As Jonathan Wolff of Oxford University wrote recently of the Research Assessment Framework: 'it has incentivised researchers to monetise their individual efforts by concentrating on documented publications to the neglect of teaching, or, indeed, devoting weeks of their lives to improving the manuscripts of their colleagues.'[11] The government has made a similar, equally unpopular, attempt to judge and regulate teaching. Coupled with the pensions dispute, and bloated salaries of managers, there is now a widespread sense that universities 'are losing their way'.[12]

Apart from some uneasy commentary in the wake of Michael Gove's decision, in March 2016, to remove parents from school governing bodies in favour of 'high skilled' professionals it is a long time since we have heard powerful voices in politics and media defend the idea of democratic school governance.[13] There are, however, a few far-sighted figures within the profession, such as the academy trust leader Ros McMullen, who anticipated the multiple problems of a 'newly academised system [that gives more] control to the Department for Education. But they cannot run schools. So instead we have the Education Funding Agency trying to do so via contracts, and, through over-regulation, killing the autonomy of leaders and creating much unnecessary and draining workload.'[14]At the same time, large academy trusts, operating right across the country, clearly undercut the principle of the local management of schools.

With growing problems of inefficient governance, undemocratic practices, and multiple and confusing lines of accountability, public attention is turning back to the core question: who should run our education system? According to an *Observer* editorial, 'converting huge numbers of schools into academies has not achieved anything other than removing them from local democratic accountability. There is no evidence that, on average, academy chains do any better at managing schools than the local authorities they replaced.'[15] Moreover, as the chief executive of an academy chain run by the Royal Society of Arts has observed, 'The notion that this small group of founding members "own" a publicly funded school or group of schools in the same way that the founders of a business own a privately established company is problematic.'[16] (The RSA invites everyone who subscribes to the charity to be a member of its trust.)

Frequent changes in government direction have be-queathed a structural mess, opening up profound gaps in accountability and governance. As one head teacher said to me, in despair: 'We cannot really call it a system any longer.' Most primary schools and a significant number of second-ary schools remain within the maintained, local authority framework while academies and MATs are directly answer-able to the Department for Education, through an opaque network of regional school commissioners – advised by a head teacher board that meets in secret and takes 'scant minutes' – headed by the national schools commissioner. Some schools now face double doses of inspection: from Ofsted and the national schools commissioner.

As perceived conflicts of responsibility and interest abound at every level, there are growing calls for reform. Influential groups like the Heads' Roundtable plead regularly for some sort of 'system coherence'. The education specialist Warwick Mansell has concluded that 'the regulation and governance of the academies sector continues to strike me as … dysfunctional, and, in the way that intervention happens when things go wrong, untransparent. These major public sector reforms, still rolling out across England as governing bodies opt, sometimes under pressure, for academy status, have been built on very shaky foundations.'[17]

Last but not least, there is widespread agreement – but not nearly enough despair or commensurate political energy – at the successive failure of governments to provide a viable route for the 50-plus per cent of young people who do not go down the increasingly troubled universities route. I discuss this at greater length in Chapter 4 but the bare facts are these: funding for further education has shrunk by a quarter in the five years since 2013, and the number of students aged over nineteen in further education or skills training has slumped from 4 million to just 2.5 million in 2016/17. Leading expert Alison Wolf has declared our further education system to be 'in tatters'.

Those on the right and left would agree. Ruth Davidson, leader of the Scottish Conservatives, has recently called for much more effective vocational education while Patrick Ainley from the University of Greenwich argues that the 'vocational route remains an inferior option that leads nowhere, as trades and crafts collapse into digital outsourcing'.[18] Ainley dismisses schemes such as 'government-backed pseudo-work placements, bogus apprenticeships and interminable internships', pointing instead to the need to invest in sustainable employment.[19]

The slowing of migrant labour into England since the Brexit vote of 2016 has spurred government to try, once again, to remedy the vocational deficit. The apprenticeship levy, which came into force in April 2017, is charged to larger businesses – those with a payroll over £3 million – and will be put towards the costs of a digital apprenticeship training scheme. In spring 2017, the government announced the introduction of 'T levels', a scheme to enable sixteen- to nineteen-year-olds to study in fifteen sectors such as hair and beauty and construction, although they must take out a loan in order to do so. By spring 2018, the pilot schemes for the first three T levels in education and childcare, construction, and digital had been delayed until 2020, with full roll-out postponed until 2023, following corporate and civil service concerns at the procurement process and content of the new qualifications.

PART TWO

From the Ground Up

3

Can We Really Afford Free Education?

The whole people must take upon themselves the education of the whole people and be willing to bear the expenses of it. There should not be a district of one mile square, without a school in it, not founded by a charitable individual, but maintained at the public expense of the people themselves.

John Adams, 10 September 1785

Britain might be substantially richer than it was forty or fifty years ago but the national narrative is that organisations once energetic and growing are now unaffordable. The overriding moral imperative is to lower allegedly insupportable taxation, not to create public goods or sustain the institutions that bind.[1]

Will Hutton, 15 April 2018

Free education, we are told, is an impossible dream in today's deficit economy. So let's start by reiterating the principal reasons why it is so important.

The first is moral: free education is a powerful message from the nation to itself, and to each one of its citizens. Education is not just part of the backstory of celebrated individual advancement but a foundation stone of the public good, a way of the nation investing in itself over the long term. Imposing costs on education reorients individuals into buyers considering wares at the market, forever weighing up the exact value of each transaction.

The second reason is political: free education is clearly of the greatest benefit to those on low incomes, liberating them from anxiety concerning the cost, in all senses, of acquiring qualifications or even embarking on learning just for the sake of it. As Alan Tuckett, former CEO of the National Institute of Adult Continuing Education, recently told the House of Lords, 'Public provision at low or no cost is a key route to significantly widened participation.' Charges, costs and fees represent a genuine block to the accessing, and enjoyment, of education at every point along the journey.

The third reason is more practical: once charges are imposed as a 'reasonable contribution' to the costs of an enterprise, how long before those costs become unreasonable, or unbearable, whatever the promises of the politicians of the day? About twelve years in the case of university fees. First imposed in 1998, at £1,000 a year, interest free, by 2010 they had jumped to an eye-watering, unreasonable £9,000, and they currently stand at £9,250 with students charged 3 per cent plus the retail price index in interest payments on their loans throughout their life. These sums may well rise further. The average graduate debt is £46,000 but, absurdly and unjustly, rises to £57,000 for students from lower-income backgrounds, who must, with the abolition of maintenance grants, also borrow to fund living costs during their degree.

In theory, no one pays for education in England up to the end of secondary phase. The reality is rather more complex. As the average cost of childcare is currently £122 per week for a part-time place and £232 for a full-time place, early years provision is hugely expensive and unsupportable for most families.[2]

One of New Labour's most successful policies was the introduction of Sure Start centres across the country: nurseries and early years settings where parents and children could access free care, learning and advice. At its peak, in August 2009, there were 3,632 centres with more than half in 30 per cent of the most disadvantaged areas. On taking office in 2010, David Cameron promised to protect them. But over the next seven years, early years provision bore the brunt of cuts to children's services. According to a recent National Audit Office study, Sure Start budgets in England were reduced by 50 per cent (£763 million) between 2010 and 2017. There is a long-running debate about exactly how many Sure Start centres have closed in the years since 2010, but the most impartial evidence base, put together by a team of researchers at Oxford University, puts the figure at a thousand.[3]

Despite overseeing these cuts, the Coalition Government became increasingly sensitive to parental unhappiness at the growing cost of childcare, particularly among more affluent families. In 2015, the Conservatives pledged to increase free (subsidised) childcare from 15 hours to 30 hours for all parents of three- and four-year-olds. However, by the time the scheme was ready to be rolled out, in the autumn of

2017, the New Economics Foundation was already reporting that significant underfunding was forcing nurseries to pay staff below the minimum wage (approximately £7.30 an hour) and parents were having to pay additional charges for services such as activities and food, hitting those on low incomes the hardest. Some providers claim that they are at risk of closure, as their business becomes unsustainable.[4] Labour's shadow minister for early years, Tracy Brabin, expressed concern that managers would trim staff pay even further, as a way to cut costs, thereby further compromising the quality of care on offer.

Similarly, while there are no upfront fees charged to parents in primary or secondary education, there can be hidden charges. Some schools set demands that come with a price tag such as requiring a particular uniform from a particular supplier as a way of weeding out poor families from applying for a place. With rising funding pressures, parents are increasingly being asked to make contributions to their children's school. In some cases this is clearly being used to enable relatively affluent families to gain a place at high-performing state schools.

In March 2015 it was reported that Grey Coat Hospital, the Church of England school where both David Cameron and Michael Gove sent their daughters, requested payment from parents of £96 when their children joined Year 7. Students hoping to go into the sixth form were also asked to contribute £120 a year, with prospective students told that, 'Paying [into the] School Fund is an important way of showing us that you are serious about taking up a place with us in Year 12 in September.'[5] Such ad hoc demands, with all the pressures they place on low-income families, are no doubt going on around the country – but they do not yet amount to anything approaching general practice or a formal policy.

However, the debate on parental contributions intensified in April 2018 when Sir Andrew Carter, head of the South Farnham School Educational Trust and chair of the government's independent review into teacher training, told the Academies Show (an annual gathering of academy providers in London) that school leaders need to take 'a radical approach' to deal with underfunding, and ask parents to help contribute to running costs, including being directly asked for cash to meet general shortfalls in school budgets. When challenged, Carter declared, 'Parents pay for schools anyway through their taxes. If every child at your school paid £1 a day you would have £60,000 more a year. That gives you two members of staff to teach. Or you go along struggling.' Schools, he said, face the choice of asking central government for more money or approaching 'the people who pay central government directly for the money'. Drawing parallels with the retail trade, he went on: 'I don't know any area of England where there is a shop in a street that says, "You are from a poor home, therefore these groceries will be free" ... Can we say we will reduce our offer to what we are given or do we just keep adding to our offer and reduce the quality?'[6] This is a highly dangerous route to go down.

Since 2010, public attention has been focused on the rising costs of a university education, even though charges for further education and adult education courses, such as the Open University, have also risen.

The original justification for the loan system was that it still provided education free at the point of delivery: the money simply needed to be paid back, over thirty years, once earnings had reached a certain threshold of income (recently increased from £21,000 to £25,000 a year). Advocates of the scheme point to the rise in applications to universities as proof of little or no damage done and the fact that most students will never pay off the massive loans that they take on, as if such a high level of default is a marked merit of the system. This position does not explain, nor justify, the precipitate drop in applications from part-time and mature students, many of them women, who appear to take a more realistic or risk-averse view of debt.

There is now widespread anecdotal evidence of the cumulative practical and psychological stresses of the loan scheme on most young people who go to university. Saddled with so much debt so early in life, only higher earners are able to take on further obligations in the form of a mortgage, at least in their twenties and thirties. Could any better way have been devised to control younger citizens and to encourage them to conform than to put them in hock to the state from the age of twenty-one, especially if their degree is in a subject or from a university that does not automatically yield a well-paying job at the end of it?

How, then, should things be done differently?

The Labour Party's promise in 2017 to abolish tuition fees tapped into the enormous reservoir of anxiety, even among the relatively affluent, about the ratcheting price of a university education. The party's relative success in that same election, particularly among the young, had an unexpected effect. Suddenly, politicians from all parties were united in agreement that the university funding system was, if not completely broken, in serious need of repair.

Even, the chief architect of New Labour's education policy, Andrew Adonis, who had initially supported the idea of fees as a 'sensible individual contribution' to the cost of education, was swift to condemn his own previous position. Adonis was also vocally critical of what he deemed to be the absurdly inflated salaries for vice-chancellors of England's universities.[7] In early 2018, Theresa May – clearly worried at the haemorrhaging of younger voters to Corbyn's Labour – announced a major review of funding for university education. However, the terms of reference make clear that the current fees structure will remain fundamentally intact, with only a little tinkering around the edges permitted, while the press speculate about a possible reduction of university fees to £6,000.[8]

Labour made a number of broader promises on education spending in its June 2017 manifesto. In relation to early years, for example, the party promised 'significant' capital investment, including the phasing-in of subsidised provision on top of the free hours currently on offer, to extend the thirty free hours to all two-year-olds and some one-year-olds and make the move to a qualified, graduate-led workforce. It also pledged to increase the wages of staff working in early years provision (among the worst paid in the education sector) and enhance training opportunities.

Some quibbled with Labour's figures. An Education Policy Institute analysis of education promises made in all the parties' 2017 manifestos claimed that there was a £1 billion a year shortfall in terms of the early years pledge while others argued that the manifesto pledge to raise £11.2 billion to cover the costs of future tuition fees does not match the £15 billion currently raised in loans.[9] Others believe the abolition of fees will largely benefit affluent students who go to better-off universities and earn more post-university.

It is, of course, vital that all promises are carefully costed and properly justified. Given the particularly high costs of expanding higher and further education, and Labour's promise to provide these free at the point of use, are there other workable alternatives to the blunt dichotomy of punitive fees versus what might be deemed an unaffordable 'free ride'?

One idea might be to publicly fund university teaching in part from taxation and in part from a National Higher Education Endowment (NHEE). The NHEE would be a non-governmental public body run by a board of trustees. In this scenario, graduates would pay an annual levy to the fund, progressively scaled (from a very low starting point) to yield more from higher earners. This system makes clear that graduates cannot 'pay' for the costs of their own education as those costs have long since been incurred and covered; rather, they make a contribution to the future costs of maintaining a national higher education system. Furthermore, this contribution is not paid directly to individual universities, as this replicates many of the ills of the present 'market' system.

Another proposal, developed by researchers at the National Institute of Economic and Social Research (NIESR), outlines an 'all age' graduate tax: seeking a small percentage of tax revenue not just from those who graduate now or in the future but from all graduates in the workforce. Such a tax, the NIESR argues, could not only 'pave a way out of the current quagmire of student debt but, in the interests of inter-generational equity, it must be applied to university graduates of all ages, not just recent and future graduates'.[10]

The advantage of this system is that it reduces the claim on general tax revenue by imposing a retrospective hypothecated charge on those who have 'benefited' from a degree over the course of their lifetime. Annual tax payments under the scheme would be considerably lower than the current repayment levels of student loans, but the scheme would provide a more secure fiscal foundation for higher education finances than currently exists. For example, a tax levied at 2.5 per cent of taxable income for all employed graduates in England would yield more than twice as much in annual revenue as is currently received from loan repayments made by English-domiciled graduates. The revenue built up in this way would be similar to the National Higher Education Endowment fund, and could be used to write off the accumulated debt of students not covered by Labour promises of a future amnesty on fees.[11]

Inevitably, a number of practical questions arise from this scheme: would all graduates have to declare themselves to the HM Revenue and Customs? If the charge is retrospective, what counts as a modern graduate? Does it apply to those educated overseas? There is no reason why such details could not be ironed out with further consideration.

Another interesting idea currently proposed is for 'learner entitlements'. Lifelong learning experts Tom Schuller, Alan Tuckett and Tom Wilson suggest a National Learning Entitlement [NLE], which applies both to the funding of further and higher education. Under the NLE, students would get access to two years' funding for a degree. For FE learners funding would be at a more generous level than at present. Anyone wishing to take a more expensive course or take up a further year of study could apply for this in the form of a loan.

In a report for the Education Policy Institute, Alison Wolf also proposes a single lifetime tertiary education entitlement covering both technical and university education. In *Remaking Tertiary Education* she envisages this entirely as a loan arrangement to be taken in whatever instalments an individual pleases, whenever they wish, and used at any approved tertiary institution. The maximum value of this would be based on the total amount that the government currently sees as appropriate for a three-year full-time bachelor's degree.[12]

The idea of an entitlement, simply understood and easily accessed, is a good one, but one which could be adapted in order to cut out the loan entitlement entirely. The cost of an undergraduate degree could be met out of revenue raised by the graduate tax while state subsidy, raised out of the general taxation, could finance vocational or adult courses. One positive effect of this might be to rebalance both our education system and our economy away from an obsession with the university path back towards adult and further education.

When Dame Sally Coates, former head of a successful London academy and now director of academies at United Learning, was asked by then education secretary Michael Gove to look into the condition prison education, her conclusion was surprisingly radical:

> What it's taught me is we need to put far more resources into school. Do we have the money to meet special needs? Do we really meet mental health problems? Do we really give good alternative provision to children who just can't cope in the mainstream or who are so difficult that we have to permanently exclude them?

No we don't. We need to put resources into that because otherwise they end up in prison, costing the taxpayer £30,000 a year, and their needs are still not met.[13]

In other words, beyond the urgent need to make good the current funding deficit in our schools there is a strong, if now rarely made, argument for substantially increasing the amount of money we spend on education in the longer term. In order to create a genuinely high-quality National Education Service, we must invest in proper early years provision, spacious school buildings, well-paid teachers, generous special needs provision, and fully resourced further and adult education, not just to prevent failure further down the line but in order to reap the multiple rewards of a service that works for all.

One possible way to make free education more palatable (as well as electorally appealing) might be to earmark funds for different stages and sectors from clearly differentiated portions of the national budget, so that a clear line can be drawn, say, from a slight increase in corporation tax (still leaving England with one of the lowest rates in Europe) to proper subsidy for a range of early years provision.

This, in effect, would transform education from a public cost into a public asset, to which the relatively powerful and affluent in society would be asked to contribute: a move from 'tax and spend' to the more nuanced narrative of 'tax and support'. Labour has made a start on this approach – suggesting VAT on private school fees in order to fund free school meals for all primary school children. Some of this revenue could be used to increase funding for primary and secondary schooling in general.

Why not go further and set up a Building Human Capital fund in order to finance a high-quality NES? This could be established, and presented, in a similar way to the £250 billion National Transformation Fund suggested by the Labour Party in its 2017 manifesto, only revenue could be drawn not from capital borrowing but a tax on capital transactions. There are various ways this could be done. As originally conceived, the Tobin Tax (named after the Nobel Prize–winning economist James Tobin) was a proposal for a small charge levied on spot conversions from one currency into another. Some advocate a tax on high-frequency share dealing. Or what about a nominal fee charged for every share sale or purchase? In *Utopia for Realists* Rutger Bregman suggests 'that if we imposed a transactions tax – where you would have to pay a fee each time you buy or sell a stock – those high frequency traders who contribute almost nothing of social value would no longer profit from split-second buying and selling of financial assets'.[14] The EU has long been in favour of such a tax, but it has been thwarted by strong pressure from the English financial services industry.

If any such tax could be enforced, it would raise billions for the Treasury. It would be much easier to justify, politically speaking, if it was clear that revenue was to be specifically channelled into investment in education. Financial capital for human capital: a fair trade-off and a sensible rebalancing of national economies in a time of irresponsible speculation, austerity, falling incomes and growing inequality. Building Human Capital proposals for expenditure could be phased in over the parliamentary term, with allocations made for repairing school buildings, investing in geographical areas that need it most, boosting teachers' and early years workers' pay, cutting back class sizes and closing the gap in per-pupil funding between the state and private sector.

4

If at First You Don't Succeed …

There is, perhaps, no branch of our vast educational system which should more attract within its particular sphere the aid and encouragement of the State than adult education. How many must there be in Britain … who thirst in later life to learn about the humanities, the history of their country, the philosophies of the human race, and the arts and letters which sustain and are borne forward by the ever-conquering English language? … The appetite of adults to be shown the foundations and processes of thought will never be denied by a British Administration cherishing the continuity of our Island life.

Winston Churchill, 1954

'Cradle to grave' is a lyrical term; it helps us picture education as the broadest of highways along which we can all travel at our own pace. However, under more forensic scrutiny, the phrase boils down to three highly pragmatic and urgent questions. First, how do we make good on the widely understood significance of the early years to later educational and life achievement? Second, how do we establish a meaningful and affordable vocational path for those who do not go down the academic route? And third, how do we guarantee far greater provision of second, third and fourth life chances to adults who did not benefit from formal education the first time round?

To expand on these points, given the relentless attention accorded to the early years within the social mobility narrative, this element of a lifelong entitlement may be a relatively easy political sell, particularly as it dovetails so neatly with the pressing needs of working parents. It is when one looks at the provision for those past the age of sixteen who do not take the university route, or older people unwilling to take on high levels of debt, that we grasp the real failures of recent times and the need for a new national consensus.

Looking at what has happened to both sectors in recent years, the findings are grim. Since 2011, while university budgets have risen by 25 per cent, mature student participation has plummeted by more than 60 per cent. Over the same period, further education budgets have fallen by 24 per cent, with more than a million adults lost to publicly supported provision, contributing to a drop of almost two million adults overall between 2005–6 and 2016–17. As provision has fallen, so has the infrastructure around further and adult education and the motivation and money to mount national campaigns to encourage adults to participate in the services that remain. Cuts precipitate a downward spiral and the public loss of memory at what was, and still could be.

Alison Wolf, who has undertaken two major investigations of vocational and technical education over the past decade, has described the funding arrangements for both further or higher education as not 'fit for purpose'. She points out that British sectors with high-skill needs such as construction and health sciences rely on importing labour, but that supply is now under threat from the likely impact of Brexit. Despite this, she says that while there is 'a network of further education colleges, with which local employers were once deeply involved [that offer] hundreds, possibly thousands, of technician and higher-level vocational qualifications [we do not have] many [students] taking them'. Instead, FE colleges are now dominated by sixteen- to eighteen-year-olds studying full-time in classrooms, with no access to hands-on work experience or a realistic chance of a job at the end of it. In England, in 2016, a grand total of 4,000 people in further education achieved a technician-level award, down from 4,900 the previous year. That is less than one in 10,000 of the population.[1] What will happen when the now ageing skilled workforce retires? We will face gaping skill shortages.

The recently introduced T levels and the apprentice-ship levy are attempts to redress the balance. Labour has also made further and vocational education a priority by pledging to do away with fees and loans, together with the abolition of the requirement that already stretched schools should contribute to the apprenticeship levy. Instead, it urges schools to work with employers through its new regional industrial strategy. It has not explicitly stated what it will do with the university technical colleges and studio schools (a form of free school) set up under the Coalition, both of which provide vocational education for fourteen- to nineteen-year-olds. There is evidence that these institutions are faltering and, as I argue later, we might be better off providing for integrated education up to GCSE year, with distinct pathways only clearly delineated after age sixteen.

The other related absence at the heart of policy is what is now called lifelong learning or adult skills (the two are not necessarily the same). We are all living longer; although there are regional and class variations, most of us can expect to live to our mid- or late eighties. More than one-third of the UK workforce will be aged over fifty by 2020. And while the government predicts that 13.5 million jobs will be created over the next ten years, with only 7 million young people coming into the workplace these extra jobs will be taken by older citizens. Unfortunately, many of these so-called jobs will be low-paid, temporary and insecure: both the employment market and the language that describes it have been disfigured, particularly by austerity.[2]

Here, too, the introduction of fees, for both vocational and non-vocational courses needs to be reconsidered. The number of adults involved in further education has slumped from 50 to 15 per cent, a drop of over 500,000 aged twenty-four or more, and there has been a fall in the adult skills budget of 35 per cent.[3] In 2016, the OECD placed the UK on the bottom rank of European and OECD league tables for skills and work-based training.[4] Unsurprisingly, adults from working-class backgrounds are less likely to take advantage of the scarce resources that already exist, while middle-class young people, who fall at the first hurdle, are often given second and third chances with the help of family.

In a culture often unhelpfully obsessed with secondary education, successive government policies have roundly neglected adults from disadvantaged backgrounds who, given the right financial and other support, would be eager to acquire skills, qualifications and professional experience.[5] We need to address the dangerous dwindling of such services, and offer help for adults both to train, retrain or 'upskill', or to take part in non-vocational adult learning. It also makes sense to concentrate greater resources on adult citizens as we already know that a significant percentage of teenagers do not make it through the secondary years successfully and will need access to training and learning later in life.

One of the dispiriting developments of recent years is that governments of all political stripes have turned away from the Churchillian view of adult education as a public good in itself and sought to justify it largely in terms of 'economic benefit' to the nation. This is short-sighted policy-making as all the evidence suggests that continuing to learn is good for individuals' health and mental health and for the communities in which they live. Furthermore, the broader the subjects and courses on offer, the richer our culture becomes.

Challenging the idea of adult learning as offering 'economic benefits' as against social ones, Alan Tuckett has observed,

> A distinguished Maori educationalist recently told me he was impressed by the way colleges in the UK help people to learn how to do things. He was, though, puzzled by the things that they didn't teach: how to be a good family member; how to relate to your community; what stories to tell your children. With an education like this, he wondered, 'Who would want to come to your funeral?'[6]

Britain has a rich history of adult education. John Bynner's useful survey of the development of lifelong learning reminds us that 'adult education goes back to the founding of Toynbee Hall at the end of the 19th century and the establishment in 1903 of the Workers Educational Association. Such advances were given a boost post-First World War by the Adult Education Committee Report, produced by the Ministry of Reconstruction (1919).'[7] According to the report, 'The experience of voluntary bodies has shown the necessity for the recognition of the peculiar needs of adults and for methods of education and methods of organisation and administration appropriate to the satisfaction of these needs.'[8] Literature, too, gives us a strong sense of the flavour of working-class auto-didacticism from figures like Leonard Bast in *Howards End* to the skilled artists from mining communities portrayed in Lee Hall's *The Pitmen Painters*.

The Open University, set up in 1969, transformed the landscape of adult learning. Even today, despite feeling the chill wind of austerity and the market, an OU graduation ceremony is an extraordinary event as students of all ages take to the stage for a celebration of their achievements. As a public event it has a more collective and generous feel than more conventional graduation events, where young men and women stride across the stage in order of their degree class, and motivational alumni speakers assure them of a secure place in the unwelcome job market. Here, the hall cheers adults of every age, some with severe disabilities, many of them having spent years, often in challenging circumstances, working towards achieving their undergraduate degree, master's or doctorate.

We need to hold on to our shared memories of more collective efforts to provide and sustain adult education:

powerful examples of the public good. Through the 1970s and '80s the Inner London Education Authority (ILEA) offered a network of provision, Education for the Whole Community, via a mix of polytechnics (five in all), further education colleges and adult education institutes for different learning purposes. By the end of its life in 1990, the ILEA was laying on 20,000 classes with 240,000 enrolments – 14 per cent of the non-vocational adult education in England and Wales for 5 per cent of the population, in which adult education was described as the 'jewel in the crown'. For thousands of people, 'Access Courses' supplied an effective bridge from early school leaving to higher education.

Reforms from the late Thatcher period onwards changed the landscape irrevocably. At that time, the government started to take central control of polytechnics and further education colleges, dividing up qualification- and non-qualification-bearing parts of adult education, leaving the latter with local authorities. This period also saw the end of the ILEA, a reflection of the Thatcher Government's fear of, and disdain for, self-confident metropolitan authorities. Extramural courses put on by universities also declined after 1992 and have almost entirely collapsed in the last few years.

According to John Bynner, four major reports in the late 1990s – Dearing, Kennedy, Fryer and Moser – all heralded 'in varying degrees, not only a changing lifelong learning agenda in favour of economic priorities but new means of resourcing it, including, in the case of Dearing, recommending for the first time, the charging of fees'. The shift to a more economistic, vocational programme was best summed up in a characteristically pragmatic but sadly short-sighted speech by Alan Johnson in 2006, when he was Labour's education minister:

More plumbing, less Pilates; to subsidised precision engineering not over-subsidised flower arranging, except of course where flower arranging is necessary for a *vocational purpose!* ... Tai chi may be hugely valuable to people studying it, but it's of *little value to the economy.* There must be a fairer apportionment between those who *gain* from education and those who pay for it – state, employer or individual. Surveys show that adults agree they should *pay more for courses where they can.*[9]

Some opportunities for adult education and retraining still remain. Union Learn – a partially government-funded initiative to help unions help their members retrain – has remained relatively robust. The Open University still exists although recruitment fell by 30 per cent between 2010–11 and 2015–16.[10] Just as income inequality has widened, so has access to cultural capital. Institutions such as University of the Third Age (U3A), a network of self-managing learning cooperatives established in the UK in the early 1980s, provide course-based education for up to 600,000 adults 'no longer in full-time employment' and there has been a growth in commercial and non-commercial Massive Open Online Courses (MOOCs) but these, like U3A, tend to favour those who are already educationally confident or experienced. And, as with many forms of distance learning, completion rates are very low.

So what needs to be done?

We could start by listening to those with long experience and knowledge. Published in 2009, Tom Schuller and David Watson's *Learning Through Life* drew on the findings of a specially assembled commission, arguing from 'the premise that the right to learn is a human right, connected with emancipation. Deliberately broad and pragmatic in scope, the report imagined 'a society in which learning plays its full role in personal growth, prosperity, solidarity and local and global responsibility', with the authors' aim being 'to set an agenda for lifelong learning that will make sense for the next quarter-century'. In 2014 they revisited their original goal to see how much – or little – had been achieved, concluding, with typically English understatement, that the picture was 'not very encouraging'.

Many of the commission's initiatives still seem relevant: lifelong learning should be based on age not stage, with the life course divided into four stages: up to age twenty-five, twenty-five to fifty, fifty to seventy-five, and seventy-five and over. Resources should be shifted upwards, with considerably more spent on the middle and older years. Other ideas included 'learner leave' from work (in order to retrain) and 'transition entitlements' to those moving from another country (the latter proposal, along with schemes for English as a Second Language, have been politically derailed by hostility to immigration, and claimants from abroad). Individual Learning Accounts would allow individuals to build up training and skills over a long period of time.

Through these schemes Schuller and Watson urge 'stronger local strategy-making by local authorities; greater autonomy for further education colleges, as the institutional backbone of local lifelong learning; stronger local employer networks; a major role for cultural institutions; and local "Learning Exchanges": for connecting teachers with learners, providing a single information point, social learning spaces and an entitlement "bank"'.

We could go further. Schools are the ideal places to provide out-of-hours adult learning, and should be funded to put on free courses for parents, and extended family members and others in the local community. All the evidence shows that when adults decide to take up a course or acquire a new qualification, it also encourages and enriches the learning of younger people in their social world.

Each area should have a thriving further education college or two at which everyone from teenagers to new parents to pensioners can acquire a range of skills, qualifications and training. Local colleges could link up with local employers in order to get hands-on work experience, although, as Patrick Ainley points out, this must go hand in hand with 'an alternative economic framework of job creation in which local authorities and public/voluntary sector alliances [generate] employment opportunities'.[11]

This emphasis on concentrated local provision is vital. According to Nigel Todd of the Workers' Educational Association,

> When you're trying to reach adults from 'the left behind' experience teaches that they won't initially travel very far from home (ten minutes' walk if you're lucky). The WEA success story, and the same was true of the Co-operative Movement for much of its history, was built on being or going local rather than expecting people to go to a centre 'far away'. If we're going to break down the 'left behind' barriers then adult ed as a community dynamo has to have the capacity to work very locally.[12]

Despite the drive towards a new localism, national frameworks still matter. Here, Schuller and Watson recommend 'a single government department with lead authority on lifelong learning, and an independent body to check on progress. There is no sign of progress on this. Responsibility for skills ricochets around ministers, and policy silos are as entrenched as ever.'[13]

Nigel Todd reflects ruefully on the fact that the store-rooms of the WEA and other programmes 'are stuffed with project reports, materials and evaluations that just get filed away when the money ends and it's on to the next one along. A ten-year plan for adult learning incorporating opportunities to review and adjust and react quickly could be like heaven!'

5

Whose System Is It Anyway?

One of the paradoxes of the last thirty years is that while governments were promoting individualism, marketisation and personal choice, ministerial intervention in schools was simultaneously spiralling out of control.

Fiona Millar[1]

There is a particular narrative that, like so much else, has its roots in Thatcherism, and it went something like this: local authority 'control' bequeathed a generation of neglected and badly run schools. (We'll leave to one side the fact that 'control' was a completely inappropriate term for the mix of support and services that local authorities provided, after the introduction of local management of schools, from the late 1980s onwards.) True, this argument has always allowed for the odd good local authority but the dominant story line, picked up by New Labour and stirred up by the Coalition, was that the old model was broken. What did it matter, this line of cross-party reasoning went, that those who sat on the local education committee had been elected and could be re-elected or replaced in four years' time? This school, that classroom, needed attention now.

So, in response to this received wisdom, New Labour built on the city technology school model of the Thatcher years, cleaving schools away from local democracy and relying, in Andrew Adonis's words, on 'charisma, persuasion and money, not legislation and regulation' as the drivers of reform. Labour, under Blair and Adonis, set up academies, largely in troubled inner cities. These semi-independent schools were modelled along traditional lines and praised highly for 'turning round' state education even as thousands of other local 'maintained' schools continued to educate their pupils to similar standards, in well-ordered institutions with high expectations.

It was never envisaged by the New Labour government that it would establish more than a few hundred such schools. Nevertheless, the Conservative-dominated Coalition after 2010 took up this 'independent state school' model with a vengeance, finally seeing their chance to sever the connection between local schools and local government. Nearly three-quarters of all secondary schools are now academies although most of the country's 16,700 primary schools remain within the local authority framework.

For the political right, the academy and free school revolution feeds into a larger project of the dismantling of the state, returning to a more pluralist model of the nineteenth century. In the words of James O'Shaughnessy, an adviser to David Cameron when he was prime minister and now a Lord and health minister, 'the period of municipalised control of schools in the twentieth century, which began in earnest with the 1902 Education Act and became dominant after the Second World War, is the historical aberration ... the point where the pendulum swung towards state control.' Even Thatcherism dared not do more than add in a few more grant-maintained schools to the mix. It took Michael Gove, and the 2010 Academies Act, to seriously start to break up the arrangements of a century.

Such a move has played into the growing depletion of local democracy itself – a self-fulfilling prophecy that has developed predictably and depressingly through the austerity years. As local authorities have had their budgets cut and vital jobs have disappeared within local authorities (some individuals moving over to leadership posts in academies and trusts), local democracy in general, and local educational leadership in particular, has come to seem like a threadbare thing: neither vital, nor efficient. This makes it much harder to argue for the return of key educational functions.

In its place, a different kind of accountability has come to substitute for local scrutiny and support. From the late 1980s Ofsted and league tables were introduced to shine the spotlight on schools that were underperforming, and while the new transparency brought some improvements it also set in train a number of dangerous practices, encouraging an unseemly and unfair competition between schools. As a consequence, a host of other factors – socioeconomic context, rootedness in a community, a broader curriculum – have dropped out of the public conversation, in part because these achievements can't be as easily tracked as data. At the same time, the growth of several powerful academy trusts – often set up by wealthy individuals with philanthropic intentions – pose a direct challenge to the local state. These organisations are, in some measure, outside democratic discourse: directly accountable to the secretary of state, and the law of results.

One has only to look across the Atlantic to see what might happen if we continue to allow a proportion of our schools to operate largely outside democratic control. Charter schools, and the increasingly combative figures that front them, appear to be a law unto themselves, deploying an evangelical language of social reform in order to justify everything from standardised testing, increased workload for teachers, radical exclusion policies, virtual schooling and a no-excuses behaviour policy. As Diane Ravitch observes, '"Reform" is really a misnomer, because the advocates for this cause seek not to reform public education but to transform it into an entrepreneurial sector of the economy [and its] roots may be traced to a radical ideology with a fundamental distrust of public education and hostility to the public sector in general …[it is] really a "corporate reform" movement, funded to a large degree by major foundations.'[2] Schools are run like businesses, the responsibility for outcomes placed firmly on teachers' shoulders, with little reference to the impact of widespread poverty, inequality or ethnic segregation. It is worrying to watch elected politicians helpless in the face of such passionate calls for 'efficiency' in the name of this conception of social justice, constantly pushed by a well-resourced, cunning and aggressive PR machine.[3]

As I outlined in Chapter 2, public, cross-party and media criticism is building at the manifest defects of our current fragmented and incoherent system. It is, however, much trickier to think through radical and feasible solutions. The current government seems only to be able to fix the worst excrescences of the 'independent state school' experiment while barely holding together the two contradictory accountability systems: one, governed by company law, the other controlled by public law; one, largely administered through local authorities, the other overseen by the national schools commissioner and eight regional school commissioners and their mushrooming staff, accountable only to central government.

However, at the time of writing, attempts are being made by more progressive groups to think through reform of a system that some even believe might well be on the point of collapse by the time of the next election. Spring 2018 saw the beginnings of a Parliamentary Labour Party inquiry into school improvement, oversight and accountability. An earlier report by the former education secretary, David Blunkett, commissioned by Ed Miliband in 2014, sought to bridge the gap between academies and the maintained sector by creating a new network of regional directors of school standards, empowered to intervene directly in all schools, whatever their type, and to respond to parental concerns about a particular school. The left-leaning think tank the Institute for Public Policy Research (IPPR) made a similar proposal in 2014, advocating locally appointed school commissioners at the city and county level, responsible for key functions from commissioning schools to overseeing school standards, and making sure all schools work under a shared framework. Others have come up with creative ideas for eliminating or moderating blatant bad practice and inefficiency – from related party transactions to lack of transparency to overlapping accountability systems.[4]

Such proposals go some way to dealing with the problems, but not far enough. The legal and pragmatic challenges of rolling back the market revolution in state education are formidable, but the key principles to apply seem to be as follows.

First, to create as level a playing field as possible in the core areas of governance, admissions and curriculum.
It is not right that some schools be allowed, in effect, to pick and choose who they will educate, a practice most recently encouraged by the granting of greater admissions freedoms to academies and free schools and leading, in some cases, to the refusal to accept or unwillingness to retain 'hard to teach' or poorly performing children. All schools must play their part in promoting a more cohesive society. It is also manifestly unfair to impose a national curriculum that many see as unimaginative and constraining, and then make an exception for nearly three-quarters of secondary schools in the name of 'innovation' and 'autonomy' – freedoms that have, as it happens, been little used. Many schools within MATs now have far less freedom than schools did before the introduction of the local management of schools in 1988: a rich, if unappreciated, irony of the current landscape. All schools should have the same rights, the same responsibilities and the same level of autonomy.

Second, we need a more meaningful definition of democratic accountability – or legitimacy.
In a 1986 report, the Association of Education Committees spoke of 'a long-sustained belief that the effective distribution of powers in the administration of the education service is an essential condition for freedom in a democratic society'.[5] In other words, dispersed powers are one guarantee of transparency, and the securing of public support.

Within such a framework, there is no place for schools run by largely unaccountable individuals and organisations, often operating under the direction of a handful of powerful trustees. School governance should include representatives from the local community, including parents, local councillors, community and business figures.

Third, funding must be fair.

This is not just a question of national government working out a 'fair funding' formula for schools in different regions and in differing circumstances but also a question of checking the growing habit of differential funding through private means. Some academy chains can call in considerable amounts of extra funds through philanthropic, corporate or church donations, as well as secure financial favours from government, such as beneficial land deals.[6] As the current funding crisis deepens, schools or academy chains with access to powerful and wealthy benefactors are appealing for additional huge sums but as executive head Duncan Spalding asks: 'How easily would a similar venture work in Stoke, or Blackpool? ... There just aren't enough billionaires to go around ... It is iniquitous.'[7] Selective philanthropy replicates and magnifies existing inequalities and makes the job of local schools, reliant on national government per-pupil funding alone, harder still. The distribution of funds should be equitable, genuinely fair and transparent.

How then should a government, concerned to create a more publicly accountable education system, act in relation to reform of academies and academy trusts (including free schools, studio schools and university technical colleges) and the restoration of what is described as 'local strategic partnerships'? The obstacles here could be legal as much as political. Academies and multi-academy trusts are engaged in a complex contractual relationship with the secretary of state, with varying freedoms and conditions attached to the contract depending on when they were created. Some have argued that the model cannot be dissolved until these contracts, requiring seven years' notice, have come to a natural end. Others believe parliamentary supremacy could be relatively easily reasserted.[8] If such contracts could not be immediately overridden, government might begin by repealing the relevant parts of legislation – principally the 2011 amendments to the 2006 Act that require all new schools to be academy or free schools, and the 2016 Act that requires forced academisation of any school judged to be failing.

In *Academies: The School System in England and a Vision for the Future,* Anne West and David Wolfe make a number of important proposals for dealing with current incoherent arrangements. These include restoring to every school genuine autonomy, including its own separate legal identity; imposing the 'requirement for parental, staff and community involvement in all schools[, which] would at least ensure a common framework for all publicly-funded schools'; shifting contracts currently held with the secretary of state to local authorities (thus restoring an essential element of localism); and 'designing a bespoke mechanism' by which a school could 'take the further modest step of being a maintained school' again.[9]

West and Wolfe's proposals offer an ingenious series of first steps for reform that go some way to countering common objections to reform of the academy model, that is to say that further structural change would be unnecessarily costly at a time of ongoing budget crisis or enormously disruptive after years of government-driven turbulence. Even so, moves towards the imposition of a common model of public education would demand political nerve and require the establishment of an independent body to handle ongoing negotiations concerning the eventual, and smooth, integration of academies and free schools back into a common framework. The current role of faith schools could provide a model for transition (although these, too, would be subject to reforms to admissions arrangements, governance and funding).

Almost inevitably, the political mood music would be hostile. Here, we might learn something from New Zealand's Labour government that decided in early 2018 to phase out its own charter school experiment (the schools much smaller in number) and immediately faced a barrage of emotional criticism about denying poorer children opportunities and returning them to a so-called failing public school system.

As for a new framework for twenty-first-century public education we could begin with a simple reaffirmation of the relationship between national and local education. 'A national system, locally delivered' was the model of the post-1944 settlement, and in many places, to this day, it still works well.[10] The same arrangement cannot be exactly reproduced, but we do know that most of the problems that have beset our system have resulted from remote authorities – be it national government, its appointed representatives or Ofsted – either failing to spot problems or rushing in to premature judgement. In contrast, the best outcomes have often resulted from close, sustained, local collaboration, such as the London Challenge secondary school improvement programme of 2003–2011, which, combined with relatively generous per-pupil spending, is considered partly responsible for the transformation of the capital's schools.

There is a clear and pressing need for certain functions to be returned to an elected authority. These include planning for provision of school places: ensuring fair admissions, building new schools where needed and preventing new schools popping up in areas of surplus capacity. Such tasks may be best performed by local authorities (which would require additional budgets in order to restore school-related expertise) with a larger regional body assigned to ensure that every area was able to deliver a full NES offer, including further and adult education, and liaising with local employers to develop a regional economic strategy including the provision of well-paid, genuine apprenticeships.

A new 'middle tier', as suggested by both the IPPR and Blunkett review, based around the new, devolved greater authorities in Manchester, Birmingham, and so on, would be easier to sell, politically speaking. However, while more local in character than the Department for Education or the Education and Skills Funding Agency, larger administrative areas such as these could yet prove to be too remote to monitor and intervene successfully in struggling schools or successfully co-ordinate other local services, from health to social services.

One of the lessons of recent years has been how both necessary and successful school-to-school support and, in particular, the creation of partnerships between schools, within a single geographical area, can be. To encourage this, even within small local authorities, would ensure that no school could become an 'orphan' (or SNOW) nor be allowed to flounder for any length of time. Schools would, in effect, be under the watchful eye not just of their own governors, but of the partnership or trust to which they belonged, as well as the local or regional authority. A more locally based inspectorate, geared to anticipate problems and offer support rather than rush in to judge, would provide further ballast (as I argue below). There is no reason why locally based academy trusts could not initially work in this way (subject to the reforms outlined above), eventually integrating fully into a common system, with larger multi-academy trusts, currently spread across regions, eventually broken up.

As I have indicated, England needs to decide whether to go further down the US road in which two kinds of 'public' education are perpetually set against one another, or finally to learn the lessons of our European and island neighbours such as Scotland and Wales, which have refused to cut the cords with local democracy, and devised reform, with varying levels of success, within this model. It is not too late for us to decide once again to administer public education through a reflective and responsive local state.

Such a determination would potentially allow the creation of a bigger and fresher *vision* for all sectors of education: fairer, yes, but more engaged, more exciting.

When the province of Alberta in Canada was faced with the growth of charter schools and the intoxicating narrative of parent choice, its democratically elected school boards called parents together and asked them what they wanted from their local schools. On being told that parents and students wished for greater flexibility in terms of courses provided, the boards created more individual pathways within their schools to satisfy parent and student demand. The boards also rotate head teachers around schools in a district to reinforce the sense of all the schools in an area working together rather than competing with each other. All of these are interesting examples both of democracy and collaboration in action.

To give a further example: while the original notion of free schools struck a chord with many communities, in reality very few parents or teachers have gone on to set one up. Most are now established by existing providers, faith groups or academy chains. However, there should be room, within a responsive democratic framework, for parents who genuinely wish to set up a new school to work with the appropriate education authority to set one up. The 1944 settlement enabled such a process and several schools were set up in this manner under previous Labour governments. It just was not trumpeted as much or, indeed, at all.[11]

Finally, there is another angle to the accountability issue that diminishes the importance of results per se, and high stakes inspection. Why not establish a more local inspectorate whose job it is both to keep schools under friendly scrutiny and offer them ongoing support? Annual reports could incorporate a far broader set of measures, beyond exam results, concerning school quality; something New Labour sought to do in the latter years of government, under Gordon Brown's premiership. I remain sceptical about how much official bodies can, or should, assess student 'well-being' or 'institutional happiness' but I see no reason why such reports could not tell us more about the school counselling service, school trips, the school orchestra, and so on, and canvass parental and student opinion on the quality of education provided. (And why not get the students themselves to produce it?)

Brian Lightman, the former general secretary of the Association of School and College Leaders (ASCL), now works as a consultant for a large academy chain. In his visits to schools, he is often party to discussions about problems that the school faces and about which they can be open with him, as he is not Ofsted. He said, 'They can say to me, "I'm really worried about this. It's not going well." You cannot say that to an Ofsted inspector because you are scared you are going to end up in special measures or whatever. Yet some of those conversations are really powerful.'[12]

Lightman thus identifies two fundamentally different approaches to school improvement. One is shaped by ideas of 'liability and culpability' and based on 'blaming head-teachers and governors for [poor] school results', sacking heads and teachers if things go badly and bringing in new people to run schools which encounter problems. This is the system currently operated in England and in the United States in particular. The other, however, offers support 'to struggling institutions, with sackings taking place as a last resort, and where even struggling schools with pockets of good practice could see these being celebrated'.[13]

Is it time to phase out Ofsted – quietly damned in a report from the National Audit Office in May 2018 – and introduce a more effective and collaborative body? How about establishing a Local School Support and Improvement Office (LOSSIO – it has a good ring to it), which could collate information on school quality from local inspectors and become the focus for ongoing discussions on national benchmarks of school quality? Certainly, it is time to end the threatening and counter-productive practice of inspectors swooping down on schools and judging them on paper trails and ever-shifting exam criteria, destabilising too many head teachers in the process.

At the same time, assessment of student progress need not be undertaken by a battery of expensively run national tests that too often undermine heads, teachers and pupils, and cause increasing stress to all. As I argue in the following chapters, a change to the ways that students are examined and judged should shift attention away from results as the only, or indeed chief, measure of how good a school is. Add to this a more robust system of teacher education and school leadership support and we might be on our way to a workable system in which everyone can breathe a little more freely.

Universities are historically autonomous institutions, but as change has been imposed on the sector at such a rapid pace, the need to protect higher education from political interference has taken on new urgency. This doesn't make universities political institutions in and of themselves, but, as with the law, undue outside interference soon becomes a highly political question. Different groups within the sector are now reflecting on how more democratic methods of governance might work to protect the historic mission of higher education, which is to leave its members free to think. Reflecting on the Bologna statement – a set of principles drawn up in 1988 and reaffirmed in 1999 to guide European universities, including those in the UK – Stefan Collini hints at a different approach to current arrangements: 'Viewed from the everyday experience of a British university two decades later, these principles can ring hollow. "An autonomous institution"? Barely a month goes by without a new diktat issuing from Whitehall and its satellite agencies. Governance is as constrained as policy. One recognised expression of autonomy is for academic staff to have a say in who is appointed to the roles of deans, pro-vice-chancellors, and vice-chancellors. In British universities – unlike the majority of their European counterparts – that doesn't happen.'[14]

The recent university lecturers' strike has spurred similar question, as to who runs universities, how genuinely democratic they are, and how governance arrangements might be altered. Why should vice-chancellors not be elected from within the academic community rather than head-hunted from beyond the borders of the university or from abroad? Such a gentle reform might constrain some of the more outlandish decisions of administrators as well as the seemingly constant capitulation to government on every demand concerning teaching and research. In a recent answer to the government's most recent green paper on higher education, a group of Goldsmiths' academics produced 'The Gold Paper'. This argued for the election of key posts within the university and proposed representative councils, academic boards and relevant subcommittees, and the replacement of the current warden's ad hoc Open Meeting with a more formal General Assembly, which would allow all staff to have an official voice.[15]

6

Return of the Professional

Today, teaching is no longer a private endeavour that takes place in a classroom. Now teachers are required to create a paper trail that proves learning has happened, for people who were not present in the room at the time … This audit culture means that, in many schools, the teacher no longer is able to decide how to prepare and deliver lessons, mark pupils' work, and assess and record learning.

Rebecca Allen, Caroline Benn memorial lecture, November 2017

There is probably no area of current education policy where successive governments have made such a crass mess of things than in the way we train, treat and reward today's educators. While we are constantly told that the improvement of our system does not lie in questions of structure or funding but is largely down to the talents and determination of individuals in the classroom or the lecture hall, nonetheless official policy works with equally depressing consistency to undermine the creation of a highly skilled, confident, well-paid and autonomous profession.

The growing crisis in recruitment and retention in the schools sector is inevitably a result of the longstanding cap on public sector pay and the incremental rise in workload. In a survey conducted in April 2018 by the National Education Union, 80 per cent of those asked said that they had seriously thought about leaving teaching over the previous year because of the long hours now required of classroom teachers.[1] A 2018 report by the National Foundation for Educational Research found that teachers' hourly pay has decreased by 15 per cent in real terms since 2009/2010, although the report found most teachers were still happy with their income.[2]

Politicians and the public may be familiar by now with these issues, but their cumulative impact is a cause for alarm. A 40 per cent drop in applications for secondary school teachers to start in September 2018 has been described as the most serious crisis in teacher training applications since the turn of the century. There has also been a significant fall in the numbers applying for postgraduate primary teaching routes. Certain areas in London, the South East and the East of England are particularly badly hit, with chronic shortages in some subjects such as science, maths, geography and modern foreign languages. Once a job deemed happily compatible with raising a young family and the enjoyment of life itself, teaching today demands long hours comparable with a profession such as law with little of the latter's status or material rewards. As Mary Bousted of the National Education Union observes, 'How can we make this job doable full-time?' Within the universities, academics increasingly protest at inflexible working conditions, low pay and, among female and BME academics, unchallenged institutional sexism and racism.[3]

Dig a little deeper beneath the familiar headlines – capped pay, long hours, insufficient funding for education itself – and the problem can be recast in more profound, human form. This is a profession subject to a worrying lack of autonomy concerning its daily conditions of work. The National Education Union would like to negotiate an upper limit on teachers' hours but as General Secretary Kevin Courtney argues, 'It's one thing preparing exciting lessons for kids. It's very different working unfeasible hours preparing evidence for bureaucrats ... we need to get back to teachers controlling their own work.'[4]

Brian Lightman, former head of the Association of School and College Leaders (ASCL) agrees:

> One of the words that I constantly hear is 'powerlessness'. People are feeling a lack of control ... They are implementing things that they do not own, they did not decide themselves ... When you talk about workload, and all the stuff that people should not be doing, it's not about the [amount of it], it's about the underlying culture ... There's a massive issue in addressing the underlying culture that affects education at the moment.[5]

It is not hard to see why teachers feel this way. As politicians have increasingly determined and directed what teachers should do and how they should do it, professional autonomy has, by definition, been eroded. The job itself has become less about open-ended discovery, in partnership with learners, but largely about delivery of predetermined outcomes. In schools, the designated task is often 'teaching to the test', funnelling knowledge in bite-size, easily digestible, exam-friendly form. There is little opportunity to innovate and experiment, or to deploy initiative or

imagination. In a new book on school autonomy, researchers Mel Ainscow and Maija Salokangas speculate that this
could be the direct result of the policy and methods used
to 'turn around' difficult schools. While initially leading to
rapid improvements in results and school behaviour, after
a while,

> a narrow, standards-driven culture and highly regulated policies
> limited teachers' pedagogical decision-making [and the] over-
> hanging fear of failure in examinations was seen to make staff
> reluctant to become involved in any form of risk-taking, even
> though there was evidence of considerable collaboration amongst
> the staff.[6]

For school leaders, keeping a close eye on individual teachers has become part of the job of monitoring school quality,
and rooting out poor performance. Yet it is impossible for
any head to do this, even if they wanted to. As Rebecca
Allen observes, 'A headteacher cannot know what is going
on in a classroom unless they are there. School leaders
need to learn to live with this uncomfortable truth and stop
asking for lesson plans, performing book scrutiny, reviewing marking and collecting tracking data. All of which
means learning to trust teachers again.'[7]

School leaders also face uncomfortable dilemmas in the
face of today's draconian accountability measures. The
ASCL has set up a commission on ethical leadership, in
order to explore some of the conflicts heads feel in terms
of the language common in today's schools ('relentless',
'laser-sharp') and their own more personal, and moral,
compass. Echoing the findings of Ainscow and Salokangas,
some heads initially lauded as 'aspirational' and 'innovative'

have not always continued to succeed, yet find it hard to return to more sustainable, human ways of determining pupil achievement. Head teacher Carolyn Roberts puts it as follows:

> We should be more confident in our own judgement. As adults we know what makes for a good society and what we want for our own families. At home most of us try to model honesty, love, wit, good temper, accountability, justice, magnanimity, reciprocity, duty, service, hope and all the virtues of a good life, tricky as it might be. We know that wealth and status don't amount to strength of character and that kindness is more important than dominance. Right ambition is – well – right, and better than the other kind. We forget the dreadful example that the timidity and box-ticking behind our blustering and swaggering sets the young. We hope fervently that someone, somewhere is telling them a better way to live.[8]

If head teachers can't model the right kind of ambition, refuse bluster and box-ticking, then who will? And if not now, when?

Historically primary and secondary teachers have traditionally required formal training. In the summer of 2012, I was taking part in a discussion in Edinburgh, on the day that Michael Gove announced the government's decision to allow unqualified teachers into England's classrooms – I still recall the sense of agitated surprise that the announcement provoked. In the years since, the number of unqualified teachers has risen exponentially. By late 2016, there were 24,000 unregulated teachers working in England's classrooms.[9] The Labour Party claims that 613,000 pupils in state-funded schools in England have been taught by adults with no formal teaching qualifications.[10]

Some of the most impassioned arguments for unqualified teachers have come from the private sector. Anthony Seldon, former head of Wellington College, now vice-chancellor of the University of Buckingham, England's first private university, supported the move on the grounds that 'becoming a teacher is not like becoming a doctor or a vet ... The teacher's role is ... more akin to that of parent ... Parents pick it up as they go along, and that's exactly the way great teachers are forged.'[11]

Seldon may have failed to grasp the demands of teaching in many state schools, compared with the private sector (or indeed universities) – demands that have proved too much for some. In October 2013, Annaliese Briggs quit after only four weeks as head teacher at Pimlico Academy, a primary school run by the Futures Academy Charity, led by Conservative minister Lord Nash. Briggs had no teaching or leadership experience whatsoever. Later in 2013, Discovery New School in Crawley, West Sussex, one of the first twenty-four free schools to open in 2011, was closed down: five of the school's seven teachers were unqualified.

Untrained staff are being put in front of, or in charge of, our children at all stages of their education. According to the Education Policy Institute, increasing numbers of childcare and early years education staff are unqualified, but are employed partly as a way of keeping costs down.[12] Before losing her job as education secretary, Justine Greening proposed a new role of teacher apprentice, with schools encouraged to employ would-be teachers at £3.50 an hour: barely £7,000 a year.

A significant development in recent years has been the shift from university teacher training, a sector which was judged outstanding at the end of New Labour's term in office, to a more fragmented, schools-based set of routes into the profession. There are now no fewer than sixteen separate routes into teaching. The original rationale for this was probably political and spelled out, if in rather crude form, by the writer Robert Peal, who declared that 'university education departments, the temples of progressive education, are in the process of being, *if not cleansed, significantly challenged* ... Indoctrination in child-centred ways at a university department is no longer a prerequisite of becoming a qualified teacher'.[13] One of the most highly praised, and publicised, teaching schemes of recent years has been Teach First, the programme modelled on Teach for America, in the United States, which takes graduates from 'top' universities and puts them into the classroom after only a few weeks of training.

More experienced voices grasped the true meaning, and long-term impact, of the shift away from requiring proper qualifications for teachers. As Chris Husbands, former director of the Institute of Education, wrote, describing a visit to Singapore where teacher education has improved through the establishment of a National Institute of Education, 'no-one could believe what we were doing in terms of deregulation'.[14]

In *Education Under Siege*, Husband's predecessor at the Institute of Education, Peter Mortimore, cogently explains why an extended period of teacher education is so important. Becoming a good teacher requires understanding of 'how children develop/how humans learn/how subject knowledge can be adapted for children of different ages/

how pupils with special needs can best be supported ... as well as awareness of the latest research on learning, and the history of education'.[15]

In place of a nationally determined, common route of teacher education, a buzzing marketplace of organisations and groups has sprung up – offering teachers a chance to get together and share good practice (see for example ResearchEd, WomenEd) or providing institutional support and the chance to gain further qualifications (such as the Institute of Teaching and the Chartered College of Teaching). The leaders of many of these organisations are often highly effective and upbeat proselytisers for their profession and it is noteworthy the excitement around the possibilities of teaching that they generate. They are not, however, best placed to deal with deeper, structural problems or discontents.

Francis Gilbert, an experienced classroom teacher and co-founder of the Local Schools Network, is adamant that the job is about 'so much more than being a trained craftsman. It's about becoming a professional who must deal with a multitude of complex situations ... it's a mode of being.'[16] Gilbert also counters the Seldon view that unqualified teachers bring a fresh 'dynamism' to their practice. He believes very particular skills are needed to face a 'difficult inner-city class' with all its challenges, while an 'untrained' or inadequately trained teacher, 'might well resort to the idea of discipline, handing out detentions or just shouting'.[17]

At the same time, a similar sense of powerlessness now besets those teaching in universities. A good university teacher is required to do very different things to a classroom teacher: he or she should, ideally, draw on their subject knowledge and research expertise and, formal lectures apart, teaching work is ideally done in small enough groups in which to explore different aspects of their specialism. University teachers are not required to keep control of large groups or to adapt the teaching of their subject to a broader range of learners. According to Cambridge academic Sarah Colvin, however, the job is changing:

> Academics and academic-related staff have historically accepted relatively low pay in exchange for autonomy, job security and a decent pension … over the past decade [university managers] have gone about replacing trust and autonomy with a culture of control, and job security with 'flexible contracts'. Another bond broke when management teams learned the language of academic-bashing, legitimising control by speaking of professional intellectuals as if they were feckless children who couldn't be trusted.[18]

To add insult to injury, the new Teaching Excellence Framework (TEF) seems to measure just about everything *but* teaching excellence. Using the designation of gold, silver and bronze, the TEF includes a range of largely irrelevant metrics or tests outside an individual's control. These include the amount of contact time that a student has with academics, the physical and digital resources of the department or university, and the likely progression to paid employment and subsequent size of graduate earnings.

It is hard to see how anyone can judge the effectiveness of tutors on courses in, say, psychoanalytic therapy, philosophy or poetry in terms of the jobs to which students may or may not progress or whether they acquire a well-paid position. Perhaps the hope is that these courses will just wither away, as they have no significant impact on the economy?

What seems certain is that these metrics will have an impact on what subjects the particular university has to offer. More recently, the government has floated the idea of the Gross Teaching Quotient, measuring teacher 'intensity' (an odd term) by a batch of yet more unreliable measures.

Making the arguments for a well-paid, properly trained profession, with automatic access to meaningful professional development, should be one of the easier tasks of a National Education Service, particularly as we face a looming crisis in terms of getting teachers into our schools and retaining them, and with politicians apparently helpless in the face of the fragmented provision that they helped to create. Do parents want their children to be taught by a stressed, underpaid or even untrained teacher? What student at university would choose to sit in overcrowded seminars run by a harried doctoral student? Who wants their baby or toddler cared for by unqualified, low-paid staff? None of this is the fault of the individuals concerned, who work as imaginatively and creatively as they can within current institutional limits.

We need, then, not only to restore a measure of respect and independence to the teaching profession, but to improve their pay and status so that they are indeed on a par with other professions such as doctors and vets. We could start by looking at how countries that truly value their primary and secondary teachers choose to train them: countries such as Finland, which has a highly competitive selection process, educates all its teachers to masters level, offers them substantial and ongoing professional development, and trusts them to do their job, without undue scrutiny or monitoring. In Singapore, teacher education (a better word than training) has been returned to a National Institute, with agreed national standards. Is it now time for us to restore teacher education to universities, working with a locally elected authority, to decide on placements? National pay and conditions should be reinstated and 'performance related' rewards outlawed.

More urgently, we need to get the right teachers to the right areas and schools right away. There are severe shortages of teachers in pockets around the country, particularly in poorer coastal areas and inner cities, and in key subjects. A National Education Service could take a countrywide overview of the crisis in supply and demand, and ensure that qualified teachers were immediately encouraged, through generous packages, to go and teach for a set period of years in those areas and subjects. Teach First, which has so successfully utilised the youthful evangelism of the relatively privileged, would be perfectly placed, in the first instance, to supply or direct the workforce to those areas where they are most needed – as long as they could ensure that new recruits stayed in place for a substantive period of time, and did not leave too soon in search of more lucrative or less challenging posts.

PART THREE

Future Perfect

7

Changing the Conversation

Today, social mobility means a scramble for the few jobs that offer security. Educators are expected to identify and help those intelligent enough to merit a top university place and top job. But there's no robust measure of intelligence, which is now widely accepted to be situation-specific and to develop throughout life ... In an unequal society, those with something to lose do everything to maintain advantage for their children.

Selina Todd[1]

As I have argued, a new educational settlement does not require the setting up of overbearing new structures; rather it involves a profound shift in how we run, fund, judge, link and ultimately improve the various institutions that are broadly in place. Part of the process of renewal goes beyond policy-making and requires us to have an honest conversation about overall aims and objectives, including recognition of what education can and cannot do.

Looking back at the modern history of our system it is

possible to chart the constant uneasy movement between education as a defining facet of a welfare state, oriented by universalist aspirations, and a much more individualist model of what schools and universities are for. The first conceives of education as a public good; the second of education as the golden ticket: a way up, a way out. This is not to take the emphasis off the individual and how they perceive or enjoy their learning. One of the ironies of the current emphasis on social mobility is that it has brought with it a kind of mass/factory model while the kind of education associated with broader conceptions of the public good is often experienced as more personally stimulating and absorbing. However important and interesting these distinctions are, the bald truth is that whatever the justifications for the approach of recent years, it appears that standards have neither significantly risen within state schools, nor are poorer children doing significantly better. Of course – as Fiona Millar points out in her book *The Best for My Child: Has the Schools Market Delivered?* – one of the problems with judging the rise (or decline) of results is a set of ever-shifting accountability measures, which means one can never precisely compare like with like. Nevertheless, the evidence that exists does not conclusively suggest an ever-upward spiral of improvement. Far from it.

Robert Coe, director of the Centre for Evaluation and Monitoring and professor of education at Durham, took a grim view of the matter in his inaugural lecture:

> Despite the apparently plausible and widespread belief to the contrary, the evidence that levels of attainment in schools in England have systematically improved over the last thirty years is

unconvincing. Much of what is claimed as school improvement is illusory, and many of the most commonly advocated strategies for improvement are not robustly proven to work. Even the claims of school effectiveness research – that we can identify good schools and teachers, and the practices that make them good – seem not to stand up to critical scrutiny. Recent growth of interest in evidence-based practice and policy appears to offer a way forward; but the evidence from past attempts to implement evidence-based approaches is rather disappointing. Overall, an honest and critical appraisal of our experience of trying to improve education is that, despite the best intentions and huge investment, we have failed – so far – to achieve it.[2]

Educational experts also seem to agree that the 'attainment gap' between children from lower-income and more affluent families has failed significantly to narrow. A recent Education Policy Institute report concluded that 'despite significant investment and targeted intervention programmes, the gap between disadvantaged sixteen-year-old pupils and their peers has only narrowed by three months of learning between 2007 and 2016. In 2016, the gap nationally, at the end of secondary school, was still 19.3 months. In fact, disadvantaged pupils fall behind their more affluent peers by around two months each year over the course of secondary school. At current trends, we estimate that it would take around fifty years for the disadvantage gap to close completely by the time pupils take their GCSEs.'[3] For 'persistently disadvantaged' children – that is, children who have been on Free School Meals for more than 80 per cent of their lives – the difference is far greater and there are, too, sharp regional differences in school and pupil performance. Unsurprisingly perhaps the recently resigned national schools commissioner Sir David Carter declared this to be the 'civil rights' battle of our age.

From this perspective, the arguments of recent decades that radical changes to school organisation, funding, the curriculum and exams are justified in terms of social mobility look weak. For too long we have been fed the mantra that if only schools got it right, then every child could escape his or her background or, at the very least, jump up a social class or two. In many ways, this scenario drew on one of the most romantic cultural narratives of post-war Britain – the poor pupil made good, thanks to the eleven-plus. Only this time, the entire non-selective system was to be given an ersatz meritocratic overhaul so that this dream could come true for the many, not the few.

During New Labour's time in office, 'aspiration' and 'meritocracy' became the favoured buzzwords, even though the use of the latter was based on a profound misreading of Michael Young's iconic, but deeply ironic, essay *The Rise of the Meritocracy*, published in 1958. The 2009 Milburn report on fair access to the professions, for example, made much of the right of parents to 'choose' a better school for their child in order to advance their chances, while failing to make clear what should happen to those unlucky enough to remain stuck in a worse one. A similar tone can be detected in many public statements about 'social mobility' from politicians across the parties and in the mission statements of organisations from Teach First to the free school movement. In many schools today, the significance and allure of Britain's top universities, and particularly Oxford and Cambridge, are constantly emphasised as if aspiring for anything other than, or different to, entry to these institutions is a failure of ambition or nerve.

This agenda is now faltering. The latest report from the standing Social Mobility Commission (SMC) has acknowledged that two decades of educational strategies to improve social mobility have not had the desired effect. As the Education Policy Institute report *Remaking Tertiary Education* confirmed in 2016, gaps between the classes remain largely unchanged. This lack of progress ultimately led to the resignation of SMC chair Alan Milburn in early 2018. He cited the failure of Theresa May's government to implement enough of the commission's proposals.

Growing economic precarity has clearly played its part, undermining the optimistic agenda that 'all can and should get on' in the officially prescribed manner. In an economy with so much unemployment and job insecurity, and with widening levels of inequality, it is unrealistic to expect underfunded schools and overworked teachers to be the chief vehicle by which all students can improve their economic chances. Bernard Barker and Kate Hoskins's *Education and Social Mobility*, an examination of two cohorts of students at high-performing academies, neatly identifies the limitations of this agenda. As Barker has observed, 'If every child got into a Russell Group university, then there wouldn't be such a thing as a Russell Group university.' [4]As more young people go to university, we see the emergence of new hierarchies, with many poorer pupils channelled into lower-status institutions but emerging with larger debts.

And what of those who fail to take the much prized 'academic' route? The one-note insistence of the political classes that young people should aim to escape the lives, families and neighbourhoods into which they are born fails them even more badly. Far better, surely, to give every child a stimulating education which might well enable them to thrive where they are. Barker and Hoskins found that parents' education and work inevitably have a strong influence on children's choices, often in a surprisingly positive sense: many young people are keen to do similar things to their mothers and fathers – as long as they are paid well and can live contented lives – rather than to escape into apparently more glamorous, challenging or wealthier circumstances.

It is also clear is that in a public service anxiously shaped around a clear set of winners and losers it is largely better off and more educated parents who manage the system best. As Diane Reay has recently argued in her book *Miseducation: Inequality, Education and the Working Classes*, many working-class children frequently feel disengaged, disregarded and marginalised in today's schools. Families of children with special needs must fight to get the provision they need on a daily basis, while official policy veers once again towards special schools rather than full inclusion.[5] Within higher education, there may well be students who act as irate customers demanding value for money and a good job at the end of their degree but far more keep their head down anxiously, keen not to screw up and have to repeat a year (another £9,000-plus, and living costs). Such conditions are conducive only to conformity, lack of questioning, diminishing enjoyment and, in some cases, severe mental stress.

Another problem with our current vocabulary of 'social mobility' is that it ignores the effect of the economy in two important ways. The first mistake is to attribute the achievements of individuals or entire cohorts to their education alone. Historic debates about selective versus comprehensive education have turned on the claim that grammar schools enabled clever boys and girls from modest backgrounds to reach their full potential and rise up the economic ladder. However, it is now well established, thanks to the research of John Goldthorpe among others, that it was changes in the economy, particularly the expansion of a professional and managerial class in the post-war years, that chiefly allowed so many from the working and lower middle class to do better than their parents. Goldthorpe has also argued that the rate of *relative* social mobility, which measures the chances of a given person escaping their class origins, has not significantly shifted for a century.[6] In recent decades our economy has stalled, with few new jobs opening up in the upper reaches of the economy. Children from middle-class and affluent backgrounds are still likely to thrive, partly as a direct result of their parents' existing privilege and extraordinary efforts to ensure that they are not downwardly mobile.

And yet schools are required to act as if anything is possible, the economy endlessly expanding, capable of offering good jobs to all who work hard and prove themselves reliable and inventive. It has become commonplace for political figures to speak of education as separate from rising inequality and poverty; a narrative that exhorts teachers to fix what in reality can only be fixed by, for example, an effective regional industrial strategy or a higher minimum wage or, indeed, a thriving public sector. Not surprisingly then, teachers feel compelled to speak out about the problems they see daily, dealing with pupils who regularly need support with food, clothes and even money. Early years providers talk of children with skin grey from malnutrition, stuffing their pockets with food for later.[7]

No one can successfully teach a hungry, cold child. Nor should schools be required to act as a social service, the first and last barrier between a faltering economy and the unrealistic demands of civil society. The new emphasis on rigid discipline in schools is surely, in part, a response to the chaos and violence of our inner cities. Yet those problems originate from far beyond the school gate and can only be fixed there. The risk is that too much tough love within schools dilutes the more exciting possibilities of education as a force for questioning and deep reflection rather than a grinding engine of survival and conformity in a hostile, unequal world.

However, we also forget the more optimistic side of the equation: what a relatively well-off economy can do, which is spend its money in wise ways, investing in the public good. As I have argued, our society can afford, within pragmatic limits, to offer our citizens a free education and a more interesting one. Thinking of education as a vital public good forces us to question long-held views about there being 'no more money in the pot' or that individuals themselves must make more of a contribution to education as a valuable commodity.

As part of this shift of emphasis, we need to be more honest about the bigger picture: the way that the constituent parts of our education system fit – or don't fit – together, forever boosting some children's chances, forever fatally constraining others. The Labour MP Dan Jarvis has spoken of how 'the daughter of a cleaner in ... Kingstone, Barnsley, [should] have the same life chances as the son of a barrister in Kingston upon Thames'. The sentiment is unimpeachable but without public honesty and structural change, it will remain just that – sentiment. None of this is an argument for static or low expectations, but it is does suggest the beginning of a serious debate on the impact of the more privileged, selective parts of our system on the rest, and a recognition of the simple fact that the elite will always find a way to reproduce itself as long as current structurally unequal arrangements stay in place.

As a further challenge to the current prevailing narrative, we need to find new ways of talking about what makes education genuinely valuable and why. Numbers may serve those such as Schools Minister Nick Gibb with his favoured sound-bite-on-repeat – '1.9 million more children in good and outstanding schools' – but they have, worryingly, come to substitute for all sorts of more complex, human judgements.

As pressures on the state system ratchet up, some seem keen to find even more dehumanising ways to dispatch the educational process. The Policy Exchange has proposed the establishment of a range of 'oven-ready resources' to provide 'coherent curriculum programmes' that, this leading think tank argues, will save teachers time, and help those new to the profession or to a specific subject.[8] Online learning could also easily become a cheap substitute for teaching. As Andreas Schleicher of the OECD has observed, the kind of rote-learning and memorisation so prevalent in England's schools lends itself far more easily to digitalisation and outsourcing to private companies.

It is important and right to mount a critique of all this, to talk of the stultification of standardised tests or the dangers of a fast food educational environment. However, it is far harder to find a language in which publicly to explore the contours of more meaningful practices and how they can be nurtured and protected.

Growing interference by government in universities has provoked a series of well-placed blows against the 'tyranny of metrics' and a more robust defence of learning for its own sake. England's universities are rightly admired around the world and our European neighbours look with confusion at recent reforms which seem to have offered little more than a dangerous lessening of academic independence. Even so, the search for a public language with which to defend what scholarship does best or even what scholarship is – particularly in the humanities as opposed to more empirical scientific or mathematical endeavours – risks sounding frustratingly nebulous or rarefied to the tougher-minded pundits or politicians.

Yet it is in the very lack of striving for a discernible outcome that education's most profound purpose might lie. Stefan Collini puts it well, when trying to define the aim of some kinds of higher education:

> Undergraduate education involves exposing students for a while to the experience of enquiry into something in particular, but enquiry which has no external goal other than improving the understanding of that subject-matter. One rough and ready distinction between university education and professional training is that education relativizes and constantly calls into question the information which training simply transmits.[9]

A vocabulary of challenge is, however, more easily deployed in relation to university-based research where the existence of specialisms, and indeed elite institutions, may create a measure of deference. It is much harder to shift the conversation at primary and secondary level, where everyone seems to possess a ready opinion of what schools should do, what knowledge is necessary, and so on. And yet, here too, success depends, to some extent, on the same commitment to uncertainty, to open-ended enquiry. In the words of one early years expert working with disadvantaged children: 'It's about being free ... it's about risk taking.'[10] Those who celebrate the cultivation of the imagination or urge creative experiment in our schools risk constant derision from the tough and worldly, their eyes on the 'ever rising standards' prize and related arguments about giving poorer children access to the world's apparently well-established and commonly agreed storehouse of knowledge. How then to put the case for greater quality without appearing to compromise 'standards' in such a toxic political climate? That is the task.

At times it can feel as if an entire history and body of practice concerning alternative pedagogies – rich, radical and experimental – has been swept away by a tsunami of targets and the need to raise the line on the graphs ever more urgently. After all, the better part of our educational history has not survived in numerical form; it can only ever be recorded as human experience.[11] Perhaps this is why adult education has, in particular, been allowed to wither away: it tends to offer no particular destination or data but is only concerned with the thing in itself – the love of Spanish or basket weaving, an exploration of the history of film noir or ancient civilisations. And yet the evidence shows that wherever later-life learning is allowed to flourish, there is a rise in individual and social connectedness and confidence.

To explore these questions more deeply, and to encourage the brave risk-takers, we need first – and last – to end what the academic Stephen Ball has called the 'discourse of derision'. As education has moved further out of public hands, it feels as if much of the conversation has shifted to the (no doubt smoke-free) back rooms, where politicians and the powerful players on the education scene meet, or into the ungovernable universe of the new media. Discussion has become much more political, in good and bad ways, with excited attention paid to 'movers and shakers', a handful of highly opinionated players, the size of twitter followings or CEO salaries. All riveting stuff except that it risks leaving out in the cold large swathes of the profession, parents, interested citizens and even elected representatives (from MPs to the relevant trades unions). Being so relentlessly of the now – this stupid tweet, that failing school – it has also accelerated a sense of the loss of large parts of our collective memory.

One could not devise a better way to diminish the confidence of the many nor stoke up the swagger of the few. As the philosopher and social critic Cornelius Castoriadis observed, 'There is no conspiracy, but everything conspires in the sense that everything radiates together, everything radiates in the same direction.'[12] Too many teachers and head teachers – feeling uncomfortably under surveillance or even under threat of losing their jobs following an unfavourable Ofsted judgement – are worryingly diminished in confidence, and disallow the evidence of their own experience or the expression of deepest held values.

More broadly, criticism or questioning itself is now considered a form of juvenile idealism or even disturbance. The resultant inhibition of robust discussion is bad not just for our education system but also for broader educational values, not to mention a poor portent the life of the nation. How can young people of the future learn to acquire the supposedly crucial four c's of the future – creativity, communication, collaboration and confidence – if the present system in which they learn is not only fatally short on every one of these qualities, but is, in fact, dominated by a hidden fifth: contempt?

8

A Passion for Learning

No one knows what the jobs of the future will be, so all people must be equipped with the ability to think for themselves, to solve problems, to make informed decisions, and to carry out the responsibilities of citizenship in a democratic society. They need a sound education, with the vocabulary and background knowledge in fields such as history, mathematics, and science, to adapt to a changing world.

Diane Ravitch, *Reign of Error*

Trawl the literature on the 'fourth industrial revolution' and the same themes repeatedly recur. We are facing the end of the job for life, the rise of the freelance, task-oriented, gig economy. In order to get ahead or even just to survive, tomorrow's workers will have to be entrepreneurial, good communicators, globally aware, thrive in solo work – 'learning to earn a living through the "start up of you"'– and skilled in teams.[1] According to Hilary Cottam, author of *Radical Help: How We Can Remake the Relationships between Us and Revolutionise the Welfare State*, we can 'expect an average of eleven jobs in a life-time ... and by 2020 half of Britons will be sole traders.'[2] Automation will rob us of millions of jobs. Manufacturing is already shifting from the factory floor to the 3D printer; coding is actually the principal foreign language of our age. Chatbots will staff call centres, but will still require human administrators and supervisors, a lonely sounding sort of job. Nano robots will enter *through* the keyhole in order to get the surgical job done. Artificial Intelligence will soon successfully be able to reproduce all the great works of art, while driverless cars will render thousands unemployed within a decade (although I anticipate a flourishing under-ground business in old-fashioned taxis, driven by surly well-informed drivers, to continue long into the twenty-first century).

Yet what most clearly emerges from this extensive liter-ature is how much more, not less, relevant and cherished the ungovernable human being, and human relations, will become in this futuristic landscape. A robot will never be able to acquire, as opposed to learn to imitate, human empathy, nor be able to instruct growing humans on how to acquire language or relational skills – genuine connected-ness, curiosity, empathy and kindness are resistant to even the most sophisticated of programmes.[3] As jobs move away from manufacturing to services, there will be more demand for stronger non-cognitive skills such as communication, confidence and resilience.

Raising children and caring for the ill and elderly may become a more central part of tomorrow's advanced econ-omies, while part-time work looks set to proliferate, and, as automation takes hold, rates of unemployment and underemployment will surely rise further. We could see creative answers to the worrying spectre of mass unemployment, such as the introduction of the Universal Basic Income (UBI). In the words of Rutger Bregman, a keen advocate for UBI, this is 'free money for everyone ... a monthly allowance, enough to live on, without having to lift a finger. The only condition, as such, is that you "have a pulse".'[4] If so, the adults of tomorrow will have a great deal more free time. Surely they will then do what humans have always done: read, think, play music, travel, cook, invent, write, swim, talk, have sex, love, gaze at the stars?

How will – how *should* – these economic and technological changes affect twenty-first-century schooling? We are told: students of the future will be able to take virtual reality tours of the planet, the human body, museums in far-flung capitals; fixed seating will disappear; there will be teamwork in corridors; students will be able to attain undergraduate and post graduate degrees from Massive Open Online Courses (MOOCs) delivered to our home terminals.

Proposals for a 'twenty-first-century curriculum' tend to put emphasis on increasing student understanding of global politics, climate change, and interpersonal relationships and fostering greater self-development and civic engagement. Such goals, unimpeachable as they are, can have a touch of non-specific windiness about them and a hint of the wrong sort of vaulting ambition as if we are setting young people the challenge to solve major problems – global warming, the fraying of democracy – that have eluded the efforts of most adults so far. Perhaps we also fear the vanishing of academic specialisms – the foundation stone of English education – into a general haze of good intentions.[5]

Returning from the wilder shores of utopian speculation to the unforgiving playground of contemporary political debate, it feels hard to know how to fit the vague future into the demanding present moment in which children must be educated daily, exams taken, specific paths in life decided. There lurks a more pragmatic fear of losing important elements of the modern scene such as an apparently new emphasis on high expectations and order in our classrooms. All schools may not yet have reached these giddy heights but such themes are understandably important to parents, and politicians are always sensitive to the anxieties of their electorate.

This nervous pragmatism may have its uses, however. In our consideration of the future we need to incorporate the right lessons from the past in the right way, to remember that our system has for too long and too often failed to provide a genuinely interesting and challenging education for most children and certainly a significant majority of disadvantaged young people. Many of the wrong turns of the past seventy years (including grammar schools, retro traditionalism and the market experiment) have stemmed, in part, from attempts, however partial, however blinkered, to rescue some, or all, from underachievement and a lack of self-fulfilment. They may have produced their own problems, but nonetheless future deliberations on curriculum, pedagogy and discipline – in the broadest sense – must stay faithful to the better part of those goals and carry forward the most fruitful lessons of the past. It is important not to underestimate any single learner or group of learners and maintain the highest expectations of all children, albeit in broader ways than currently conceived. We must take particular care to invest, in all senses, in the education of the disadvantaged and make sure that schools are seen as places where we learn how to live together in interesting harmony. Last but not least, the daily experience of education must be shot through with friendly, engaged order. We could call this approach both progressive and rigorous.

What might such a perspective look like in practice? At the heart of all these initiatives must be a renewed emphasis on the importance of nurturing relationships and capabilities of all kinds: an imperative perfectly in keeping both with the anticipated demands of Artificial Intelligence and some interesting contemporary ideas on the principles behind the revitalisation of the welfare state.[6] At an early years level, there needs to be a switch away from didactic, fact-based learning to the play-based curriculum that has been well established, by numerous researchers, as the best foundation for deep understanding, one that recognises the vital emotional and relational elements of learning. As Lucy Crehan describes in *Cleverlands*, her account of high-achieving school systems around the world, some of the most impressive school cultures delay the onset of formal learning until the age of six or seven, and put emphasis on this playful, creative model in the early years. Not only is there no evidence of ill-effects in terms of achievement by the late years of the primary stage, there are clear emotional and social benefits. Research suggests that children who delay formal education until seven years old are less likely to have ADHD at age eleven and show better self-regulation – a skill associated with improved social and academic performance in later life.[7]

Our system's current overemphasis on testing needs to be phased out in favour of different forms of formative rather than summative assessment, with teachers constantly 'feeding back' responses to students, and resources directed to support struggling learners to achieve their very best. The celebrated work of the Cambridge Primary Review team, and its network of schools around the country, showcased and celebrated numerous examples of imaginative practice. To take one example: Wroxham Primary in Hertfordshire, which Alison Peacock took over when it was in special measures. Under her leadership, Wroxham pioneered peer-to-peer collaboration, the constant encouragement of curiosity and a strong emphasis on 'oracy' – much greater emphasis on the spoken word, in every part of school life. This created not just an extremely happy school but one consistently rated 'Outstanding' by Ofsted.

At secondary level, there should be no contradiction between deep subject learning and more engaging methods of teaching. As I have argued, for many teachers the traditional/progressive divide is pernicious: a false binary. Educational researchers John Hattie and Greg Yates argue that Initiation-Response-Evaluation methods – that is, teacher at the front asking fact-based questions, soliciting and evaluating response – are the most dominant and least successful mode of teaching across the world, with no thinking or activity or real engagement on the part of the child. In contrast, we need more of what the teacher and writer Debra Kidd calls 'warming up a cold curriculum'. The work of figures such as Kidd, Tom Sherrington and Martin Robinson help to bring a sense of greater rigour and intellectual engagement to professional discussions of just how much today's schools – and pupils – can achieve. Pioneer schools such as School 21 in Newham have successfully put oracy at the heart of their work with outstanding (in all senses) results. Projects such as Learning Without Limits

– the movement that rejects fixed-ability labelling – and Slow Education point the way to further radical developments in our thinking about how young people learn.

This is not just abstract theory. There are schools around the country, often led by brave heads, that have deliberately pursued their own pedagogical path. Stanley Park High School in Carshalton, South London – named 'Secondary School of the Year' at the 2016 TES Schools Awards – has pioneered a curriculum integrating practical and academic subjects, putting strong emphasis on students taking charge of their own studying, drawing families in to greater involvement in school life, and focusing on strong and happy relationships between staff and students. One of its apt mottos is 'Igniting a Passion for Learning'. Visiting the school, I sat in on some impressive pupil-led sessions at which Year 8 students made formal presentations on what they had learned during the year, displaying project work, models or written pieces, while analysing their strengths and flaws in tremendous, emotionally literate detail. Aged just thirteen, these learners of varying 'academic' ability displayed a confidence, oral fluency and self-knowledge beyond that of most adults I know – skills which can only be of great benefit to them in all that lies ahead, be it public exams, moving into paid work or just life itself. The school sets an example in other, interesting ways as it integrates young people with varying levels of autism into all stages of the curriculum right up to A level by providing tailored social, practical and academic support to learners with special needs at all stages.[8]

Honywood Community Science School in Coggleshall in Essex puts strong emphasis on creative subjects at a time when the Ebacc – the performance measure introduced by the Department for Education in late 2010 to encourage all students to take five academic GCSEs – and other accountability measures have led many schools to reduce their offers in this area. When I visited, a number of articulate Year 10 'lead learners' explained the thinking behind 100-minute lessons and students being able to book 'time out' for one-on-one work with a teacher or mentor on any subject they felt either worried about or had a particular passion for. Year 9s gave me a taste of their recent project work, showcasing not just what they had learned and created but reflecting thoughtfully on difficulties encountered along the way. Head teacher Simon Mason explained to me how much individual agency is woven into every element and stage of learning, 'ensuring that students understand that it is the choices they make that drive their success in life rather than fixed notions of ability or social class'.[9]

At Matthew Moss High School in Rochdale, an 11–16 comprehensive in the top quintile for measures of deprivation, senior leaders also wrestle with the implications of the Ebacc. They are reluctant to force students into taking subjects that don't engage them, while clearly keen to improve on students' qualifications. A strong emphasis on enjoyment of the arts is evident on even a short tour of the school, with its airy music and art studios filled with a variety of teenagers deeply absorbed in creative tasks. Matthew Moss proudly encourages young people to find out what they love doing, and pursue it, partly through using the Slow Education method.

Mike Grenier, a teacher at Eton, and an active member of the Slow Education network, explains the thinking behind the model:

To achieve mastery of a subject requires time to learn but also time to reflect on how learning has happened. Many simple tests/forms of assessment largely remove any thinking and simply become tests of memory. Thus the so-called traditionalists rail against skills as if they are somehow nebulous and examples of lazy thinkers, and the so-called progressives see knowledge as damaging to creativity and of no lasting significance. Both positions are incorrect.

According to Grenier, however, the 'more nuanced synthesis of thinking and learning that is at the heart of Slow Education [is] hard to implement [in a] culture of "fast-food" learning in which ... measurement becomes paramount.'[10]

What most struck me about the schools I visited was their rigour. They mix something of today's 'high expectations' culture with older ideas about granting young people the time, and freedom, to learn more deeply. It is also significant that they are in areas of high deprivation or surrounded by more selective institutions, meaning a significant proportion of Year 7 pupils will arrive with a sense of demoralisation about having failed to get into a 'better' school: the curse of the English system. Yet I was deeply impressed by the degree of commitment, and self-critical reflection, displayed by heads, teachers and teaching assistants. There was plenty of what might be called traditional learning going on in both schools, but the whole point of Slow Education, or the approach taken at Stanley Park High, is not to spurn knowledge but to anchor it more authentically. Luckily, its impact can be assessed in terms of data and destination as well as in the manifest enjoyment of students. Only 1.7 per cent of students at Matthew Moss end up not in education and employment, with those who go on to tertiary college performing strongly right up to age eighteen. National figures indicate that up to 7 per cent of post-sixteen students are not in education and employment. GCSE results at Stanley Park High have also improved as a result of the intensely engaged approach taken at the school.

So, what are some of the policy implications of such a shift in approach to teaching and learning?

Education is inevitably a deeply political question, but that does not mean politicians should directly decide what children learn. Without doubt, the setting of the national curriculum should not just be removed from politicians, of all parties, but separated from the distorting nature of the political cycle itself. Nor is there a need for such a curriculum to set out in suffocating detail what knowledge needs to be acquired year by year. In *Cleverlands*, Lucy Crehan describes how the most successful countries have a lighter-touch curriculum, designed to encourage deep mastery rather than total coverage. There is far greater regional, school level and teacher autonomy in respect of implementation. It makes sense that the core curriculum should be set out, and periodically revised, by a standing committee of experienced and highly respected teachers, heads, academics and subject specialists.

At both primary and secondary level, the curriculum should be broad and multidisciplinary and, at secondary school, should involve not just a spread of expected academic subjects but ensure plentiful provision of the arts, drama, music, physical exercise, consideration of political and social questions, sex and relationship education: all those elements that the futurologists (and our own common sense) tell us is so important. Every child should have the right to learn a musical instrument and a foreign language, and given help to develop digital and emotional literacy. The philosopher John White believes time should be found within the school day or week for the full development of individual interests, whether they be in cooking, ancient philosophy, dress making or electronics. Students should be encouraged from a young age to take part in designing some part of their lessons or helping run some part of the school. At Honywood Community Science School, pupils are encouraged to take up leadership roles in the school from mid-adolescence. In this way, important human qualities – individual enterprise and creativity, collaboration and communication – are embedded as part of daily school life: habits of mind and heart learned early.

This broader approach requires a new framework of qualifications and exams, as first proposed by the Tomlinson Report of 2004. Sadly it was rejected by Tony Blair's government which did not want to ditch the 'gold standard' of the A level. More recently, the Heads Round Table (HRT), an influential group of state school heads, has come up with an idea for a 'rigorous inclusive and flexible curriculum and qualifications framework'. The HRT recognises that the current system is in a fragmented mess, with vocational qualifications post-16, in particular, extremely weak, those with special needs virtually abandoned within the current system and a lack of sufficient stimulation, opportunity and scope for learners of every kind.

Rather than create new exams, the HRT proposes a framework that can incorporate existing qualifications in an imaginative and coherent way. A 'national baccalaureate' gives equal weight to the academic and vocational, but will also contain some core, common components. All students study maths and English up to age eighteen, undertake a personal project and other non-exam-related forms of learning such as community service. In order to make the right decisions about their upper secondary school choices, future learning paths and eventual employment, students will have access to properly funded guidance and careers advice.

The new 'bacc' framework has nothing to do with the limited, and limiting, Ebacc. Under the HRT scheme, students who wish to go the vocational route can 'put together' a technical baccalaureate, while more academic learners will continue to take A levels and go the university route. On leaving school, a student will be given a transcript of all their scores and achievements that will give higher and further education institutions and employers an enriched picture of the nature and scope of their achievements and, one hopes, their very personhood.

The beauty of the scheme is that it offers a genuinely comprehensive framework for a comprehensive age. It returns, in robust realistic form, to an early aim of the comprehensive movement: to bridge the harmful and self-limiting class-based division of the grammar/secondary modern divide and create a 'common curriculum for all students'. Up to sixteen years old, most students will follow a broadly similar pathway but with more flexibility and far greater variety built in their schooling, as currently exists in countries such as Finland and Canada. With the addition of skills and special projects to the 'knowledge' component of both the pre- and post-16 period, it moves us away from the grammar school-lite emphasis of recent reforms and makes sure that schools can best serve all students.

Similar proposals were put forward in the third report from the independent skills task force headed by Chris

Husbands, former Director of the Institute of Education. It, too, suggested a National Bacc based on four learning domains: core learning (qualifications such as A levels or accredited vocational qualifications), maths and English to age eighteen, a personal skills development programme and an extended project. Some individual schools have adopted the approach more informally, such as Archbishop Sentamu Academy in Hull which offers a 'modern bacc-alaureate'. Students gather credits for everything from an extended project, community support and 'meeting a personal challenge'. The 'mod bac' allows for greater flex-ibility, enabling students to mix academic and vocational elements right up to age eighteen. For more practical skills, it checks elements of its programme against CBI employ-ment criteria, including problem-solving, team working and application of numeracy and IT skills.[11]

Currently, all these proposals, continue to incorporate GCSEs and A levels. However, it is possible, given the rise of the school leaving age to eighteen, that ultimately we will move to lighter-touch, less expensive – and less stress-ful – forms of assessment at sixteen. For the moment, these diverse initiatives offer both a coherent and contemporary framework that meets the challenges of the future and a truly national system. They can be utilised by any school in the country, whatever its mix, and balance of learners. The proposals also foster useful co-operation between schools and colleges in any given area. It works with the mass of qualifications we already have and would not be unneces-sarily expensive to implement.

9

Towards an Integrated System

Ultimately there may be no alternative to full integration into the national education system ... Fundamentally, my problem is with the fee-paying principle – which leads directly to engines of privilege, blocks relative social mobility and perpetuates a Berlin wall not just in our education system but in our society.

David Kynaston

If our international competitors think that the future is comprehensive, why shouldn't we?

Sir Michael Wilshaw, former Chief Inspector of Schools

Unlikely as it might sound, one of the most electric political meetings I have ever attended was a lecture on the Finnish educational system given by Pasi Sahlberg, the Finnish educator and author, in the spring of 2012. Sahlberg, who was speaking to a packed Committee Room 14 of the House of Commons – the most magnificent of a run of grand meeting rooms that directly overlook the Thames – has a rather laconic manner of delivery. However, in this particular instance, his flat speaking style proved the perfect vehicle for an unexpectedly radical message.

Sahlberg described how Finnish education had evolved, in the post-war period, from a steeply hierarchical one, rather like our own, made up of private, selective and less-well-regarded 'local' schools, to become a system in which every child attends the 'common school'. The reforms were partly initiated to strengthen the Finnish nation after the Second World War, and to defend it against Russian incursions in particular. Finland's politicians and educational figures recognised that a profoundly unequal education system did not simply reproduce inequality down the generations but weakened the fabric of the nation itself. Following a long period of discussion, which drew in figures from both the political right and left, educators and academics, Finland abolished its fee-paying schools and instituted a nationwide comprehensive system. Not only did such reforms lead to the closing of the attainment gap between the richest and poorest students, it turned Finland into one of the global educational success stories of the modern era.

I was recently reminded of this meeting when reading a short pamphlet published in November 1964 by the Young Fabian authors Howard Glennerster and Richard Pryke on 'the public schools' (astonishingly one of the few print publications to be found on this subject in the British Library's exhaustive catalogue). Much of the pamphlet covers the same ground occasionally trod today by the odd, brave soul: the social divisiveness bred by a parallel school system for the better off, the disproportionate access of privately educated pupils to Oxford and Cambridge and then to the top jobs in society, the dispersal of bursaries largely to the cash-strapped middle class, the numerous canny tax schemes enjoyed by both private school parents and the schools themselves that amount to large state subsidies to the most privileged in society. The pamphlet ended by dismissing the foolishness of those who say that state schools should 'catch up' with the private sector. The answer was integration.

The pamphlet also quoted the Labour Party manifesto of 1964, which promised that 'Labour will set up an educational trust to advise on the best way of integrating the private schools into the state system of education'.[1] It also included an extract from a document titled *Signposts for the Sixties*, which provided a statement of Labour Party 'home policy' submitted by the National Executive Committee to the 60th Annual Party Conference: 'We are convinced that the nation should now take the decision to end the social inequalities and educational anomalies arising from the existence of a highly influential and privileged private sector of education, outside the state system.'[2]

The Young Fabian authors concluded that 'in the future these statements may be seen to mark a turning point in the development of British education ... now Labour is committed to action, and action there will have to be'. Sadly, it was *not* to be. As David Kynaston and George Kynaston noted in a long, cogent consideration of the issue published in *New Statesman* in 2014, the Labour Party, if not the wider left, has largely remained silent on the issue of private schools for forty years.[3]

We urgently need to renew the conversation about the private–public divide, and move beyond the superficial, profoundly apolitical debates of recent years. These have chiefly been characterised by the rolling out of the same information again and again, almost as if the private schools were not human creations but unchallengeable phenomena like the weather or religious deities. Over and over we are told: private schools achieve higher results; their graduates hoover up the majority of places at the best universities; they take all the top jobs; they dominate the top of society. There is, as a result, a continual stirring up (with the liberal help of a few capital letters) of resentment, envy and panic – 'Private pupils are SIX TIMES more likely to get A* grades at GCSEs than those at state schools';[4] 'A third of private pupils score 3 A* grades at A level compared to one in TEN at state schools'[5] – finely seasoned with a good dollop of hopelessness: 'The awful truth: to get ahead you need a private education.'[6]

Moreover, many today still peddle the line that those prescient Young Fabian authors of half a century ago urged us not to take, which is to implore our often battered state system to close the widening divide through non-stop 'improvement'. During a BBC Radio Four debate on education in the run up to the 2015 general election, Fraser Nelson, editor of the right-wing weekly *The Spectator*, argued that what was needed was more visits by the influential and successful to state schools, more internships and mentoring of the disadvantaged. Useful as such initiatives might be, to some individuals, it is hard to see how such stop-gap methods will do more than chip away at a yawning structural divide.

We can't expect the Conservatives to say much about private education: after all it underwrites a hierarchical form of social organisation, and philosophy of individual freedom, intrinsic to the party's philosophy. Labour's position in the post-war period – from roughly the late forties to the early seventies – was, as I have indicated, to deplore the divide and promise to do something about it. In 1997 New Labour got rid of the Assisted Places Scheme: a system of subsidies for private schools. Yet the most marked feature of the post-1997 New Labour years has been the suggestion that state education could benefit from imitation of the autonomy, pedagogy, disciplinary atmosphere, as well as the direct patronage, of the private sector.

Under this rubric, two distinct policies were pursued. One was to lure cash-strapped private schools into the state sector, via the academies and free school movement. To date, a handful of private schools have come into state education via this route but enjoy preferential admissions arrangements and other advantages that some argue have intensified stratification within the state system.[7] The other, much heralded, path, particularly in the Adonis/Gove years, was that of 'partnership': the idea that private schools should sponsor struggling academies. Spurred on by a mix of duty, guilt, interest in innovation or some combination of all these, some schools – including Brighton College, Dulwich, Eton, Highgate, King's Canterbury, Wellington and Uppingham – joined the scheme. However, a number subsequently pulled out. As one private school head is reputed to have said, 'I take my hat off to these guys who run academies. I wouldn't last five minutes in that environment.' Former Chief Inspector of Schools Michael Wilshaw was sceptical of the arrangement, telling a gathering of private school heads that the so-called partnerships amounted to no more than 'crumbs off your tables, leading more to famine than feast'.

If we are to move the conversation on, then, we need

to be clear that the success of private education is not replicable precisely because it offers the already socially and economically privileged superior resources and opportunities that inevitably augment their confidence and capabilities in every sphere. Private day schools now cost, on average £14,500 a year – more than the annual disposable income of the average English family. Boarding is a great deal more costly. The annual fees of a top private school such as Westminster, which sends more students to Oxbridge than any other school in the country, are around £35,000 a year. Compare this to the average per-pupil spend in a state secondary school of between £4,000 and £6,000 a year. But the difference is not only in simple resources, for the spread of pupils at many state schools will include those from deprived or struggling families, compounding the pressures on their education and those who teach them, while a private school is in general recruiting from the already affluent, literate and enterprising. Thus, we need publicly to acknowledge that the success of private education is far less to do with character building or autonomous governance than the powerful alchemy of several kinds of advantage.

Now, more than ever, there is a strong moral and political argument in support of integration. At a time of growing divides and damaging inequality, we urgently need public institutions that bring the nation together, not further separate and divide us. For many in the UK the idea of a unified education system to which all subscribe is too great a leap of the imagination, too daring a proposition, yet the benefits of a common schooling could be immense. Finland teaches us not only that state education will never be considered truly first-rate until we give all our children the same high-quality schooling but that a country that educates its children together has a better chance of being at ease with itself than one which segregates different parts of the population from an early age. On a more rawly political note, the greater the spread of families using a public service, the greater the pressure on politicians to commit sufficient funds to support it. Or as David Kynaston puts it rather more amusingly: 'one only has to witness pushy private school parents on the touchline to realise that the state sector will never achieve its full capability without them.'[8]

It may be that the problem with private education is not that it is too expensive but that it is too cheap. Certainly, low-level growling about the extent of state subsidy of private schools has a long history. The Charities Act 2006 removed the presumption that charities automatically provide public benefit, and decisions on this question were shifted to the Charity Commission, which, in statutory guidance, 'ruled that people in poverty should not be excluded from the services of these "charities"; their benefits should be made available to a "sufficient" section of the population, be quantifiable and reported on annually'.[9] Since then, there has been intermittent and testy discussion as to whether the sharing of playing fields and libraries, and the provision of Latin taster classes and so on to neighbouring state schools constitutes sufficient public benefit. In 2014, Tristram Hunt, then Labour shadow minister for education, boldly proposed that private schools should lose some of their business rate relief if they didn't form more meaningful partnerships with state schools. There were even rumours, in 2017, that Theresa May would withdraw charitable status from private schools that refused to participate in the sponsorship of academies and free schools. [10]

Paradoxically, austerity may have played a part in ratcheting up the pressure on private schools. In early 2017 Taunton Deane council in Somerset initiated conversations with its three local private schools on how the latter could contribute more to the 'community benefit' of the area, through donating 10 per cent from its Business Rates Relief. According to Steve Ross, an independent councillor, private schools in the district received a tax discount of £868,060 in 2016–17, of which more than £340,000 would normally have been taken by the council through the business rates system. Ross argued,

> We recognise we have to give the schools business rates relief, but we considered the time was right to seek better engagement with the schools and see whether their delivery of public benefit could be aligned with tackling local priorities ... In an area with national pressure on education, plus county pressure on children's services and libraries, and our borough having deprived wards in which literacy is identified as a barrier to families accessing services and employment, we need to look at, and beyond, the current arrangements.[11]

The mood music is changing. In the run-up to the 2017 general election, Jeremy Corbyn proposed that VAT should be charged on private school fees in order to subsidise free lunches for all primary school children. In December of that year, the Scottish Government accepted the recommendations of the Barclay Review that Scottish private schools should lose their business rate relief, with the exception of some specialist and special needs schools.

Robert Verkaik, author of the recently published *Posh Boys: How the English Public Schools Ruin Britain*, calculates that 'the UK spends more on private education than any other country in the developed world'. Private schools could have been expected to pay £1.16 billion in business rates between 2017 and 2022: as charities, he argues, they will pay just £634.26 million, equating to circa £522.31 million in savings. Eton, for example, will save an estimated £4.1 million in business rates over the next five years.[12] Yet state schools, which are not charities and do not receive fee income, must pay the full rate. Verkaik also investigates the manner in which private schools, as charities, are exempt from UK tax on most types of investment income and do not pay corporation tax of 20 per cent, which means every penny of profit a public school makes is tax free: if this income were taxed, it could raise up to £500 million. He has also highlighted the considerable sums of money used to subsidise private education for the children of military families.[13] By removing some forms of public subsidy, and possibly taxing school fees (a report by the Fabian Society in 2010 suggested that introducing VAT on private school fees, estimated to be £9 billion, could raise around £1.5 billion annually), private education might start to become more like a luxury brand, encouraging a significant proportion of parents to choose the state sector.

Imposing further taxes on school fees is just one of several reforms that could bring us closer to a more integrated system.[14] Proposals for outright abolition are likely to raise an unproductive political outcry followed by years of legal wrangling over the rights of parents to pay for their children's education, in whatever form. The Sutton Trust has proposed an Open Access Scheme, under which the state would subsidise 25 per cent of places at top-performing private schools to those on low or medium incomes, with places allotted on a selective basis. A number of leading private schools have already indicated a willingness to participate in the scheme. However, given the overwhelming evidence concerning the social discrimination inherent in eleven-plus–style tests, such a plan would exclude the genuinely poor, further deprive state schools of motivated and high-attaining pupils, justify selection at a time when it is seriously being questioned in the state sector (see below), and bestow an additional, and wholly unjustifiable, moral halo upon private education. Earlier schemes of a similar nature, such as the Assisted Places Scheme, abolished by the Blair government in 1997, ended up largely subsidising the already educationally advantaged on moderate or low incomes.

A more radical approach might be to compel private schools to take, as their 25 per cent quota, children who have been on free school meals for an extended period of time, children who have been in care or children who struggle to reach basic levels of attainment. Any money that the state channelled to private schools in the form of subsidies for pupils such as these would amount to a form of redistribution of which few could disapprove while finally returning the private schools to their original mission, lost in the mists of pragmatic time, to educate the genuinely needy.

Given the considerable and sustained advantage that private school students currently enjoy in terms of access to top universities, and from there to the most influential and well-paid jobs, there is also a case for an increase in contextual admissions criteria – ensuring that universities take into account economic and educational contexts when offering places, particularly at so-called 'top' universities. 'Potential' is always a tricky quality to judge. In a recent blog entitled, 'Making Oxbridge Entry Matter Less', the education researcher Rebecca Allen described a period she spent conducting admissions interviews at an Oxbridge college. 'The experience completely revolutionised my view that university admissions were efficiently selecting students by ability … Those who performed exceptionally well at interview often didn't seem to turn out to be genuinely interested and motivated by their subject.'[15] (Allen knew this because she also worked as a supervisor of first-year students.) In other words, confident self-presentation may not always indicate authentic passion while, in a reverse manifestation of the same question, one state school head told me that some of his most brilliant sixth form students were not – yet – able to translate their passions into an acceptable form of fluency, but could be taught to do so.

Allen also noted that accompanying 'thinking skills' tests were clearly not tutor-proof and confirmed that disadvantaged students were often not prepared for the demands of the interview. In the long term, some of the fresh approaches to teaching and learning that I proposed in the previous chapter would, I hope, produce even greater numbers of intellectually (and orally) confident and questioning pupils, whatever path they chose to take after school. In the short term, given that exam results determine entry to all universities, there is a strong case for lower entrance requirements for those who have had a less well-resourced education, especially as research shows that state school students admitted to highly selective universities with the same A level results as their private school peers outperform the latter.[16]

Lady Margaret Hall in Oxford has recently set up a free, fully funded foundation year for students usually 'under-represented' at Oxbridge to give disadvantaged students a taster of demanding courses at an elite institution and aid applications to university entrance proper. While some might question the sensitivity of such a publicly visible separate track for those from more modest backgrounds, it is an indication of a new determination to shift entrenched inequalities. The point is that the less that private school attendance is associated with a smooth transition to a top university, the less incentive there is to parents to pay fees in order to educate their children separately.

Within the state sector, there is a less daunting transition to be managed in terms of selective education. Kent, Lincolnshire and Buckinghamshire have fully selective systems, pretty similar to those operated in the post-war period. In Birmingham, to take one example of how selection operates in the big cities, eight grammar schools cream off the most motivated and high-achieving students and make secondary transfer for all Birmingham's parents a complex, messy and socially unfair business. While there are only 163 grammars – fast expanding under this government – it is estimated that the secondary education of one in ten children nationwide is affected by the nearby presence of a selective school.

I have already discussed the divides that this creates, and the negative impact that the existing – and expanding – grammars have on other local schools. Expensive private coaching, beyond the reach of most families, is a crucial part of winning a place at a selective school. While some ethnic groups do better than others in selective systems, grammars disproportionately exclude children from minority back-grounds.[17] Selective schools are more likely to be rated outstanding as other local schools suffer, their pupil intake out of balance in terms of the proportion of disadvantaged, disengaged children – many of whom are demoralised by having failed the eleven-plus and told that they are not up to the mark – or those with special needs. It is often hard to recruit and retain teachers. These de facto second-ary moderns are more likely to be judged 'inadequate' or 'failing', and the vicious circle is complete.

Stephen Gorard and Nadia Siddiqui of Durham University have examined data for every cohort of pupils in England in 2015. They conclude that

> this kind of clustering of relative advantage [in grammar schools] is potentially dangerous for society … [taking] measures of chronic poverty and local socio-economic status segregation between schools, [we use] these to show that the results from grammar schools are no better than expected, once these differences are accounted for. There is no evidence base for a policy of increasing selection, and so there are implications for early selection policies worldwide. The UK government should consider phasing the existing selective schools out.[18]

Lobby groups as politically diverse as Comprehensive Future and Bright Blue agree with this conclusion. Comprehensive Future proposes that we slowly open grammar schools up to a fully comprehensive intake: ensuring local populations can decide the best means of transition, what use to make of existing grammar school buildings, and how to prepare teachers in the selective sector to teach all children to the highest level.

Such a move would complete the reforms of the '60s and '70s that occurred across most of the country. Change is still happening today. In 2016, Guernsey, a small crown dependency, voted to transform the island's school system, converting a single grammar school and three secondary moderns into a unified system. For decades, campaigners against selection have been patiently arguing their case, putting forward the evidence and attempting to persuade others. Finally, they won. From 2019, Guernsey will have a fully comprehensive secondary school system and join some of the most successful and modern education systems in the world. It is time England did the same.

Afterword

An education act of 2020 should be passed after a cross-party parliamentary 'conference' … Its task should be to take evidence
from all interested stakeholders about what our future education
service should look like … and provide a comprehensive action
programme for all educational entitlements, from the earliest
years into old age. It would herald an age of ambition, hope and
partnership and a society committed to unlocking the talents not of
a few, nor even the many, but of all its citizens.

Tim Brighouse, *Guardian*

In 2014, as the relatively new chair of Comprehensive
Future I was asked to address a meeting on school admis-
sion reform in the House of Commons to an audience of
politicians and lobbyists. Presenting a set of carefully prepared ideas, based on years of research, analysis and policy
discussion, I was asked, rather briskly, at the meeting's end:
'That's all very well, but do you have any nudge-style proposals that might get a hearing in Downing Street?'

That question has haunted me over the years and, perhaps unfairly, come to epitomise the fatal limitations of educational thinking in mainstream political circles in recent years. Don't look at the big picture. Give us a small, smart, relatively safe idea that the politicians might snap up.

Such an approach seems inadequate in current circumstances. It is time for boldness, for the setting out of agendas that will bring real change, and to put fresh manifestos in front of politicians and public alike. In this, I echo the recent call of Tim Brighouse for urgent reform of our system. Under the heading, 'Rab Butler revolutionised education in 1944. Let's do it again', Brighouse claims that our school system is broken and only a new act will fix it.[1] He lays out five key aims, all of which chime with the ideas I have set out: resolving the crisis in teacher recruitment and retention; reforming the curriculum; reform of the accountability system; fairer admissions; and closing the funding gap between private and public education.

To Brighouse's proposals I would add two further pressing priorities. We need a government that is committed to greater economic as well as educational equality. The OECD states unequivocally that if education is to make a real difference, fairer school systems have to go hand in hand with policies to enhance economic equality. As Richard Wilkinson and Kate Pickett point out in their most recent book, *The Inner Level: How More Equal Societies Reduce Stress, Restore Sanity and Improve Everyone's Wellbeing*, 'The larger the income differences [within a country], the more strongly children's educational performance is marked by status differences.'[2] Increased funding to state education remains an urgent matter. In the spring of 2018, teachers in the US state of Oklahoma marched for more money for their public (state) schools – many of them so poorly paid that they are having to take on one or even two extra jobs in order to teach in rundown public schools. It was an alarming portent of what might happen here: how a once proud public service could become frighteningly skeletal and unfit for purpose.

An important new conversation has begun: it's up to us all now to carry it forward in our schools, colleges, universities and localities, to educate an often woefully ignorant media, and to urge our elected representatives, at every level, local and national, to bring forward policies that will help create and sustain a modern and genuinely equitable education system fit for the twenty-first century.

Acknowledgements

A book, especially a short one, is always a collective effort. I would like to thank the following who read some or all of the manuscript in draft and gave me their comments: Stefan Collini, John Fowler, Paul Gordon, Francis Green, Debra Kidd, Gawain Little, Warwick Mansell, Fiona Millar, Tom Schuller and Nigel Todd. I am grateful to you all; naturally all opinions and mistakes are my own. Others have shared their time and insights including David Kynaston and Robert Verkaik, Anne West and David Wolfe, the board members of *Forum*, and my colleagues and fellow campaigners at Comprehensive Future, the Local Schools Network and the Socialist Education Association. Warm thanks to my patient editor Leo Hollis and my always encouraging agent Faith Evans, and last, but hardly least, to Paul, Hannah and Sarah who have kept me going with tea, tenderness and teasing.

Appendix: 'My Government Will ...' – A Proposed Short Legislative Policy Programme

- Abolish baseline testing, SATs in Year 2 and Year 6, and instead introduce a system of ongoing teacher assessment, with sample testing conducted on a random national basis.
- Abolish Ofsted and set up a Local School Support and Improvement Office (LOSSIO).
- Repeal the relevant sections of the 2011 and 2016 Academies Acts and return basic powers to local authorities: to open schools, determine and manage admissions, coordinate health, social and educational services.
- Set up a commission to consider proposals for the integration of academies and free schools into a publicly run system, and put all schools, including existing faith schools, on the same footing in terms of funding, admissions, governance and autonomy.
- Set up a new regional authority charged to liaise with local authorities to ensure that every area within its

jurisdiction provides the full NES offer of primary, secondary, further and adult education, and to ensure that every school leaver has access to full advice and support in regard to future options.

- Establish a three-year National Learning Entitlement for all school leavers, funded either from the public purse or the all-age graduate tax.
- Abolish tuition fees and set up a National Higher Education Endowment fund to administer the proceeds of an all-age graduate tax.
- Establish a Building Human Capital Fund to secure long-term investment in state education and to establish an initial set of priorities for expenditure, particularly in early education, further and adult sectors, and to raise the level of funding for our schools.
- Set up a National Teaching Force to ensure adequate teacher supply and retention in areas of shortage.
- Restore national pay and conditions for teachers.
- Abolish the Research Excellence Framework and the Teaching Excellence Framework.
- Institute a Proportionality of Pay rule in all educational institutions, including universities, so that there is a direct, and reasonably fair, relationship established between the salary of the most senior and junior member of staff.
- Set up an independent National Curriculum, Qualifications and Examinations Committee, to establish, and regularly revise, a core curriculum: to introduce a baccalaureate model to England's schools and to advise on the possible phasing out of GCSEs.
- Phase out use of the eleven-plus test over an agreed period and provide resources and expert advice to

currently selective areas, and schools, to ensure a smooth and successful transition to comprehensive education.

- Set up an educational trust to advise on the best way of integrating the private schools into the state system of education.

Further Reading

Patrick Ainley, *Betraying a Generation: How Education is Failing Young People*, Policy Press, 2016

Melissa Benn, *School Wars: The Battle for Britain's Education*, Verso, 2012

Melissa Benn and Janet Downs, *The Truth About Our Schools: Exposing the Myths, Exploring the Evidence*, Routledge, 2016

Nuala Burgess, *A Tale of Two Counties: Reflections on Secondary Education 50 years after Circular 10/65*, Comprehensive Future and King's College, 2016

Stefan Collini, *What Are Universities For?*, Penguin, 2011

——, *Speaking of Universities*, Verso, 2018

Lucy Crehan, *Cleverlands: The Secrets Behind the Success of the World's Education Superpowers*, Unbound books, 2016

Michael Fielding and Peter Moss, *Radical Education and the Common School: A Democratic Alternative*, Routledge, 2011

Susan Hart, Annabelle Dixon, Mary Jane Drummond and Donald McIntyre, *Learning without Limits*, Open University Press, 2004

Debra Kidd, *Teaching: Notes from the Front Line*, Independent Thinking Press, 2014

Fiona Millar, *The Best for My Child: Can the Schools Market Deliver?*, John Catt Educational Ltd, 2018

Robin Pedley, *The Comprehensive School*, A Pelican Original, 1963

Diane Ravitch, *The Death and Life of the Great American School System: How Testing and Choice Are Undermining Education*, Basic Books, 2010

Diane Ravitch, *Reign of Error: The Hoax of the Privatization Movement and the Danger to America's Public Schools*, Alfred A Knopf, New York, 2013

Martin Robinson, *Trivium 21c: Preparing Young People for the Future with Lessons from the Past*, Independent Thinking Press, 2013

Martin Robinson, *Trivium in Practice*, Independent Thinking Press, 2016

Diane Reay, *Miseducation: Inequality, Education and the Working Classes*, Policy Press, 2017

Tom Sherrington, *The Learning Rainforest: Great Teaching in Real Classrooms*, John Catt Educational Ltd, 2018

Brian Simon, *A Life in Education*, Lawrence and Wishart, 1998

Robert Verkaik, *Posh Boys: How the English Public Schools Ruin Britain*, Oneworld Publications, 2018.

Notes

Introduction

1. See for example: Lucy Crehan, *Cleverlands: The Secrets Behind the Success of the World's Education Superpowers*, Unbound, 2016; and Pasi Sahlberg, *Finnish Lessons: What Can the World Learn from Educational Change in Finland?* Teachers College Press, 2012.

1. The Long Road to Reform

1. Adrian Elliott, *State Schools Since the 1950s: The Good News*, Trentham Books, 2007, p. 50.
2. David Kynaston, 'What Should We Do with Private Schools?', *Guardian*, 5 December 2014.
3. Brian Simon, What future for education?, London: Lawrence and Wishart, 1992, p. 76.
4. Peter Housden, *So the New Could be Born: The Passing of a Country Grammar School*, APS Group (Scotland) Limited, 2015, pp. 77–8.
5. Paul Bolton, 'Education: Historical Statistics', Standard Note: SN/SG/4252, House of Commons Library, November 2012.

6. Melissa Benn and Jane Martin, 'The Patron Saint of Comprehensive Education; an Interview with Clyde Chitty', Part Two, *Forum*, 60:1, 2018, pp. 11/12.

7. Ibid., p. 16.

8. Becky Gardiner, 'Why I am a striking lecturer: I want to stop the slow death of public education', *Guardian*, 12 March 2018.

9. Robert Long, 'Academies under the Labour Government', Standard Note SN/SP/5544, House of Commons Library, 20 January 2015.

10. Diane Ravitch, *Reign of Error: The Hoax of the Privatization Movement and the Danger to American's Public Schools*, Alfred A. Knopf, 2013, p. 4.

11. David L. Kirp, *The Rebirth of a Great American School System and a Strategy for America's Schools*, Oxford University Press, 2013, p. 4.

12. Melissa Benn and Janet Downs, *The Truth about Our Schools: Exposing the Myths, Exploring the Evidence*, Routledge, 2016, pp. 76–94.

2. Emerging Crises, Emerging Consensus

1. See Mary Bousted 'Why force teachers to teach in a way that goes against what they believe in?' *Times Education Supplement*, 28 March 2018; Tim Brighouse, 'Rab Butler revolutionised education in 1944. Let's do it again', *Guardian*, 3 April 2018; Eleanor Busby, 'University students receive "paltry returns" for their academic degrees', *Independent*, 5 February 2018.

2. Ed Dorrell, 'The battle over grammar schools has only just begun', *Times Education Supplement*, 23 February 2018.

3. See in particular Stephen Gorard and Nadia Siddiqui, 'Grammar schools in England: a new analysis of social segregation and academic outcomes', *British Journal of Sociology of Education*, 26 March 2018.

4. See for example: 'Fisking Melissa Benn's Guardian article on free schools', Conservative Home, 9 September 2011; for a more measured exchange see Melissa Benn and Rachel Wolf, 'Free

Schools: For and Against', *Prospect*, 24 August 2011.

5. Education Select Committee report into multi-academy trusts, 23 February 2017.

6. Professor Toby Greany and Jean Scott, 'Conflicts of Interest in Academy Sponsorship Arrangements,' London Centre for Leadership in Learning, Institute of Education, University of London, September 2014.

7. House of Commons, Committee of Public Accounts, 'Academy Schools Finances', published 26 March 2018.

8. Alice Bradbury and Guy Robert-Holmes, *Grouping in Early Years and Key Stage One: A Necessary Evil?*, National Education Union and University College London, October 2017.

9. Amanda Spielman, speech at Ark's Teach 2017 conference, 27 November 2017.

10. Professor Sir Keith Burnett, 'Higher Education Green Paper: Are We All Consumers Now?', University of Sheffield, published 9 November 2015, emphasis in original.

11. Jonathan Wolff, 'Everything must be measured: how mimicking business taints universities', *Guardian*, 8 August 2017.

12. Jack Grove, 'The USS strike and the winter of academics' discontent', *Times Higher Education Supplement*, 12 April 2018.

13. Sally Weale, 'Plan to stop parent governors sparks row in schools shake-up', *Guardian*, 17 March 2016.

14. Ros McMullen, 'Tread warily in this brave new academy world,' *Schools Week*, 19 March 2016.

15. 'The Observer view on the Tories starving schools of funding,' Observer, 27 January 2018.

16. Alison Critchley, 'Academy members have too much power but it's not their fault', *Schools Week*, 8 May 2017.

17. Warwick Mansell, 'Companies or Schools? Problems of Governance in the Academies Sector', National Education Union, 28 June 2017.

18. Patrick Ainley, *Betraying A Generation: How Education Is Failing Young People*, Policy Press, 2016, p. 97.

19. Ibid., p. 103.

3. Can We Really Afford Free Education?

1. Will Hutton, 'Open University gave millions of Britons a second chance. Now it needs one itself,' *Observer*, 15 April 2018.
2. 'Average childcare costs', the Money Advice Service, online, April 2018.
3. May Bulman, 'Government "understating" extent of Sure Start children's centres closures as thousand lose vital support', *Independent*, 4 April 2018.
4. Tracy Brabin, 'Silence of the Tories on childcare shows their policy is unravelling', Labour List, 5 September 2017.
5. 'Grey Coat school chosen for David Cameron's daughter in fund row,' *Daily Telegraph*, 13 March 2015.
6. Pippa Allen-Kinross, 'Struggling to afford CPD? Charge parents £1 a week, says leading head', *Schools Week*, 25 April 2018.
7. Andrew Adonis, 'I put up tuition fees. It's now clear they have to be scrapped', *Guardian*, 7 July 2018.
8. Richard Adams, 'Theresa May to reveal details of tuition fees overhaul on Monday', *Guardian*, 16 February 2018.
9. Andy Westwood, 'The Numbers Game', in Kate Murray (ed.), *Life Lessons: A National Education Service That Leaves No Adult Behind*, Fabian Society UCU report, 2018, p. 10.
10. Geoff Mason, 'Graduates of All Ages Should Help Pay for Higher Education', posted on the National Institute of Social and Economic Research blog website, 7 March 2018.
11. Ibid.
12. Alison Wolf, *Remaking Tertiary Education: Can We Create a System That Is Fair and Fit for Purpose?*, Education Policy Institute, 14 November 2016.
13. Laura McInerney, 'Profile: Dame Sally Coates, director of academies south, United Learning', *Schools Week*, June 14 2016.
14. Rutger Bregman, *Utopia for Realists*, Bloomsbury, 2017, p. 217.

4. If at First You Don't Succeed ...

1. Alison Wolf, 'England's higher education system "in tatters"', *Financial Times*, 14 November 2016.
2. Tom Schuller and David Watson, 'Learning for Life: how far have we come?', *Adults Learning*, 26:1, 2014, p. 8.
3. John Bynner, 'Whatever happened to lifelong learning? And does it matter?,' Lecture at the British Academy, 21 March 2017.
4. Ibid.
5. See for example, Catherine Baksi, 'Denisa Gannon: Roma people are not getting justice', *Guardian*, 20 March 2018.
6. Alan Tuckett, 'Leitch cannot disguise the death of lifelong learning', *Guardian*, 2 January 2007.
7. Bynner, 'Whatever happened to lifelong learning?
8. 'Voluntary organisations and education', Chapter VII of the 1919 report on adult education, available at http://www.infed.org/archives/e-texts/1919report.htm.
9. Quoted by Bynner, 'Whatever happened to lifelong learning? And does it matter?', emphasis not in original.
10. Anna Fazackerley, 'Part-time student numbers collapse by 56% in five years', *Guardian*, 2 May 2017.
11. Patrick Ainley, *Betraying a Generation: How Education Is Failing Young People*, Policy Press, 2016, p. 103.
12. Nigel Todd, in private conversation with the author.
13. Tom Schuller and David Watson, *Learning Through Life*, National Institute of Adult Continuing Education, 2009, p. 9.

5. Whose System Is It Anyway?

1. Fiona Millar, *The Best for My Child: Can the Schools Market Deliver?*, John Catt Educational Ltd, 2018.
2. Ravitch, *Reign of Error*, p. 19.
3. Megan Erickson, 'All About Eve', *Nation*, 1 November 2017.
4. See Alison Critchley, 'Academy members have too much power but it's not their fault', *Schools Week*, 8 May 2017. At a February

2018 meeting of the Heads Round Table, Matt Hood and Laura McInerney unveiled their own detailed proposals for reform, helpfully called the 'Hood–McInerney model'.

5. Foreword to a report on local education committees published by the Association of Education Committees (AEC) in 1986.

6. Warwick Mansell, 'High-paying Harris Federation spent £12m more than it received in income, accounts reveal,' Education Uncovered, 1 February 2018, educationuncovered.co.uk.

7. Louise Tickle, 'Schools: how to raise £1m a year', Guardian, 22 May 2018.

8. See David Wolfe's submission to the Blunkett review: David Blunkett, *Review of Education Structures, Functions and the Raising of Standards for All*, Appendix III, Labour's Policy Review, 2014.

9. Professor Anne West (LSE) and Dr David Wolfe QC (Matrix), *Academies: The School System in England and a Vision for the Future*, Clare Market Paper No. 23, Education Research Group. Department of Social Policy, London School of Economics and Political Science, June 2018.

10. I am grateful to Peter Mortimore for reminding me of this crucial point.

11. Alexandra Park School in Muswell Hill, North London, now a thriving local secondary school, was set up in just this way in 1999.

12. Warwick Mansell, 'Sense of "powerlessness" affecting teaching profession, leading educationist warns', *Education Uncovered*, 26 March 2018, educationuncovered.co.uk .

13. Ibid.

14. Stefan Collini, 'In UK universities there is a daily erosion of integrity', *Guardian*, 24 April 2018.

15. 'The Gold Paper', published by Goldsmiths University and College Union.

6. Return of the Professional

1. Richard Adams, 'Vast majority of teachers considered quitting in past year – poll', *Guardian*, 1 April 2018.
2. Alix Robertson, 'Teachers are "happy with pay" despite real-terms drop', *Schools Week*, 20 March 2018.
3. Selina Todd, 'The academics tackling everyday sexism in university life', *Guardian*, 24 February 2015.
4. Kevin Courtney, 'We need an upper limit on teachers' hours', *Times Education Supplement*, 28 March 2018.
5. Warwick Mansell, 'Sense of "powerlessness" affecting teaching profession.'
6. Mel Ainscow and Maija Salokangas, 'Giving teaching back to teachers', 29 November 2017, educationuncovered.co.uk.
7. Rebecca Allen, Caroline Benn memorial lecture, November 2017.
8. Carolyn Roberts, 'Why have an ethical leaders commission?', Education Uncovered, 13 November 2017, educationuncovered.co.uk.
9. Department for Education, 'School workforce in England: November 2016', published 22 June 2017.
10. Ibid.
11. Anthony Seldon, 'Teaching is like parenting: you don't need to have a qualification', *Guardian*, 28 October 2013.
12. Sara Bonetti, *The Early Years Workforce: A Fragmented Picture*, Educational Policy Institute, March 2018.
13. Robert Peal, *Progressively Worse: The Burden of Bad Ideas in British Schools*, Civitas, 2014, emphasis added.
14. Peter Mortimore, *Education Under Siege*, Polity Press, 2013, p. 55.
15. Ibid., p.57
16. Francis Gilbert, 'Can evidence-based pedagogy raise levels of achievement?', francisgilbert.co.uk, 16 March 2014.
17 Francis Gilbert, in private conversation with the author.
18. Sarah Colvin, 'UK academics have snapped – and not just over pensions,' *Times Higher Education*, 22 March 2018.

7. Changing the Conversation

1. Selina Todd, 'Labour is right: social mobility is not a good goal for education', *Guardian*, 1 August 2017.

2. Professor Robert Coe, 'Improving Education: A Triumph of Hope Over Experience', Inaugural Lecture of Director of the Centre for Evaluation and Monitoring, Durham University, 18 June 2013.

3. Jon Andrews, David Robinson and Jo Hutchinson, *Closing the Gap? Trends in Educational Attainment and Disadvantage*, Educational Policy Institute, August 2017.

4. Bernard Barker, in private conversation with the author.

5. Sally Weale, 'Families crowdfund legal action against special needs budget cuts', *Guardian*, 13 April 2018.

6. For a full account of Goldthorpe's arguments, see John Goldthorpe, *Understanding – and Misunderstanding – Social Mobility in Britain: The Entry of the Economists, the Confusion of Politicians and the Limits of Educational Policy*, Oxford Institute of Social Policy and Nuffield College, February 2012. See also Melissa Benn and Janet Downs, *The Truth about Our Schools: Exposing the Myths, Exploring the Evidence*, Routledge, 2016, pp. 12–18.

7. Ed Riley, 'Malnourished children with grey skin are filling their pockets with school canteen food to survive in poor areas, say head teachers', *Daily Mail*, 2 April 2018.

8. John Blake, 'Completing the Revolution: Delivering on the Promise of the 2014 National Curriculum,' Policy Exchange, 2018.

9. Stefan Collini, *What Are Universities For?*, Penguin, 2011, p. 56.

10. Alex Beard, ' How Babies Learn – And Why Robots Can't Compete', *Guardian*, 3 April 2018.

11. As one small example, a former head of three primary schools and Local Authority Adviser, Geoffrey Marshall, sent me a link to his website, Alongside the Child, giving examples of the wonderful, independently conceived, artwork done by many of his pupils in the period 1972–87. See sites.google.com/site/edulectures/.

12. Cornelius Castoriadis, *Postscript on Insignificance. Dialogues with Cornelius Castoriadis*, Bloomsbury, 1999, p. 28.

8. A Passion for Learning

1. Valerie Hannon, *Education Forward: Moving Schools into the Future*, Crux, 2017, p 38.

2. Hilary Cottam, *Radical Help: How We Can Remake the Relationships between Us and Revolutionise the Welfare State*, Virago, 2018, p. 32.

3. Alex Beard, 'How Babies Learn – And Why Robots Can't Compete', *Guardian*, 3 April 2018.

4. Bregman, *Utopia For Realists*, p. 49.

5. Ibid., p. 220.

6. See, for example, Cottam, *Radical Help*.

7. May Wong, 'Study finds improved self-regulation in kindergartners who wait a year to enroll,' Stanford Graduate School of Education, 7 October 2015.

8. For a detailed description of the work of Stanley Park High, see *Forum*, 60:1, 2018, which carries a number of articles on the work of the school.

9. Melissa Benn, 'Let's Hear It for the Truly Independent Schools Bravely Rebelling Against Neo-Traditionalist Policy', *Teach Secondary*, 20 April 2017.

10. Melissa Benn, 'The slow revolution that makes learning fun', *Times Education Supplement*, 11 December 2015.

11. Skills Taskforce, *Qualifications Matter: Improving the Curriculum and Assessment for All: The Third Report of the Independent Skills Taskforce*, Labour's Policy Review, 2014.

9. Towards an Integrated System

1. Howard Glennerster and Richard Pryke, 'The Private Schools', Young Fabian pamphlet, 7 November 1964, p. 1.

2. Ibid.

3. David Kynaston and George Kynaston, 'Education's Berlin Wall: The Private Schools Conundrum', *New Statesman*, 3 February 2014.

4. Chris Parsons, 'Private pupils are SIX TIMES more likely to

get A* grades at GCSEs than those at state schools', *Daily Mail*, 3 September 2011.

5. Kerry McQueeney, 'A third of private pupils score 3 "A" grades at A level ... compared to one in TEN at state schools', *Daily Mail*, 20 October 2011.

6. Catherine Bennett, 'The awful truth: to get ahead you need a private education', *Observer*, 2 May 2010.

7. Fiona Millar, 'When private schools fail, why should the state bail them out?', *Guardian*, 11 February 2014.

8. David Kynaston and George Kynaston, 'Education's Berlin Wall.

9. Fiona Millar, 'Private schools do not understand "public benefit"', Guardian, 10 May 2011.

10. Liam Kay, 'Government says policy pledge on private schools has not been dropped', Third Sector, 13 September 2017, thirdsector. co.uk.

11. Freddie Whittaker, 'Council launches investigation into benefits of private schools', *Schools Week*, 3 March 2017.

12. Robert Verkaik, *Posh Boys: How the English Public Schools Ruin Britain*, Oneworld Publications, 2018, pp. 255–7.

13. Robert Verkaik and Tony Diver, 'Military families given £246m of taxpayers' money to send their children to private school', *Daily Telegraph*, 15 April 2018.

14. For a much more detailed discussion of various ideas for reform, see Francis Green and David Kynaston, *Engines of Privilege: Britain's Private School Problem*, Bloomsbury, to be published in February 2019.

15. Rebecca Allen, 'Making Oxbridge Entry Matter Less', 20 October 2017, rebeccaallen.co.uk

16. Richard Adams, 'Top state school pupils get better degrees than those from private schools', *Guardian*, 5 November 2015.

17. Comprehensive Future, 'Asking the wrong questions, ignoring the right answers', comprehensivefuture.org.uk.

18. Stephen Gorard and Nadia Siddiqui, 'Grammar schools in England: a new analysis of social segregation and academic outcomes', 26 March 2018.

Afterword

1. Tim Brighouse, 'Rab Butler revolutionised education in 1944. Let's do it again', *Guardian*, 3 April 2018.
2. Richard Wilkinson and Kate Pickett, *The Inner Level: How More Equal Societies Reduce Stress, Restore Sanity and Improve Everyone's Well-being*, Allen Lane, 2018, p. 171.